Also available in the *7 Lessons* series

Roger Mason

ISBN 9781399830089

7 Lessons in
Leadership
Master the Basics in 7 Steps

Dr Carol O'Connor

ISBN 9781399830119

7 Les[...]
Lead[...]
Teams
Master the Basics in 7 Steps

Nigel Cumberland

ISBN 9781399830140

Master the Basics in 7 Steps

Mo Shapiro

ISBN 9781399830164

7 Lessons in
Sales
Master the Basics in 7 Steps

Christine Harvey

ISBN 9781399830188

7 Lessons in
Persuasion and Influence
Master the Basics in 7 Steps

Di McLanachan

ISBN 9781399830553

7 Lessons in
Strategy
Master the Basics in 7 Steps

Stephen Berry

ISBN 9781399830577

7 Lessons in
Time Management
Master the Basics in 7 Steps

Robert Ashton

ISBN 9781399830591

7 Lessons in
Bookkeeping And Accounting
Master the Basics in 7 Steps

Roger Mason

ISBN 9781399830515

7 Lessons in
Customer Care
Master the Basics in 7 Steps

Di McLanachan

ISBN 9781399830539

7 Lessons in Persuasion and Influence

Master the Basics in 7 Steps

Di McLanachan

First published in Great Britain in 2016 by Teach Yourself. An Hachette UK company.

This edition published by John Murray Business in 2026
An imprint of John Murray Press

1

Paperback ISBN 9781399830553
ebook ISBN 9781399830560

Typeset by KnowledgeWorks Global Ltd.

Printed and bound in Great Britain by Clays Ltd, Elcograf S.p.A.

John Murray Press policy is to use papers that are natural, renewable and recyclable products and made from wood grown in sustainable forests. The logging and manufacturing processes are expected to conform to the environmental regulations of the country of origin.

John Murray Press
Carmelite House
50 Victoria Embankment
London EC4Y 0DZ

John Murray Business
Hachette Book Group
123 South Broad Street
Ste 2750
Philadelphia, PA 19109, USA

www.johnmurraybusiness.com

John Murray Press, part of Hodder & Stoughton Limited
An Hachette UK company

The authorised representative in the EEA is Hachette Ireland, 8 Castlecourt Centre, Dublin 15, D15 XTP3, Ireland (email: info@hbgi.ie)

Contents

Introduction

As social animals, we human beings cannot not communicate. Even if we are not speaking, our visual appearance and body language will 'speak' for us. It is therefore not surprising that people who have learned to be influential and persuasive communicators enjoy great success in life. This book will teach you how to master a range of practical and proven techniques for influencing and persuading others, which will work in all aspects of your personal and business life.

This is more than just a collection of theories on how to persuade and influence others. Spread throughout are real-life examples of people who have been acknowledged globally as highly successful influencers, together with insights into how they achieved this. And if they can do it, you can too!

LESSON 1

What is influence?

According to dictionary definitions, 'influence' can mean:

- to affect how others see a certain point or action, and react upon it
- to leave a mark on someone (not literally)
- to have someone or something start acting a bit like you.

Influencing others is one of the prime objectives of communication and is particularly important in the business world. In his 1936 book *How to Win Friends and Influence People*, Dale Carnegie wrote that dealing with people is probably the biggest problem we face, especially in business. He went on to say, 'There is only one way under high heaven to get anybody to do anything and that is by making the other person want to do it. There is no other way.'

In this lesson we will be examining some of the factors that have been proven to be effective and powerful influencers, delivered by personalities as diverse as Sir Winston Churchill and Sir Bob Geldof. We will also explore what influences you – whether you make 'head' or 'heart' decisions, and how you 'sell' yourself when you want to promote yourself to others.

What influences your decisions?

Think about the last time you bought something that was a 'want' rather than a 'need'. Perhaps you were out and about, and you just saw something that caught your eye. You liked the look of it and you decided you wanted it, even though you knew you didn't need it. You might have been aware that, at that point, a voice inside your head went into 'justification mode'. It started generating 'reasons' why you really should have this object of your desire. Before you knew it, you had made your purchasing decision, handed over some money and it was yours.

Perhaps you remained pleased with that purchasing decision, or perhaps, in the cold light of a day or two later, you wondered what on earth possessed you to hand over good money for this 'thing'. Whatever your feelings about that decision, your personality type will have influenced it.

The following is a list of different personality types related to buying decisions. Notice whether you identify with any of them.

The gadget geek

If it's the latest technology, cutting-edge design and it's considered cool to possess one of these, then the gadget geeks want it. They have an image to sustain, after all. If Apple brings out a new iPhone, then they have to be first in the queue to get one. They may even be prepared to pay someone to stand in the queue all night on their behalf so that they get pole position. They don't even need to know what new features this iPhone has: if it's new, it must be a better, improved version of the last model and it's essential for them to be bang up to date.

When the Apple iPhone5 first went on sale in London, among the people in the queue eager to part with £599 was a man who justified his purchase by telling a journalist that he had just bought an Audi A6 and it was 'only compatible with a phone that has a milled aluminium finish'! These people make justified, 'from-the-head' decisions.

The connoisseur collector

These people don't buy; they invest. They seek 'elite purchases', which they refer to as 'investment pieces'. They attend fine-art auctions or – if the item they want has a particular rarity value – they stay away and become a telephone bidder, in case their presence inflates the price. Although they love beautiful things, connoisseur collectors are also prepared to invest in items that are acknowledged as desirable and therefore valuable, even if they are not to their personal taste. These could include fine wines, which they 'put down' in a temperature-controlled wine cellar, never to be consumed.

Admiration is everything and the quality of their possessions reflects their personal aspirations. They want to be seen as discerning buyers with impeccable taste. Although image is important to this group, their purchasing decisions tend to be led by the head rather than the heart because of the investment factor.

The memorabilia collector

These people consider themselves to be similar to the connoisseur collectors but dedicated to a particular theme. The theme might be *Star Wars* merchandise, royal family memorabilia or Barbie dolls through the ages. Because there tends to be no limit to the size of their collections, they are constantly adding to them, sometimes to the extent that their collected 'treasures' take over all the space in their homes. Charity shops, car boot sales, eBay and sci-fi fairs are all happy hunting grounds for these 'from-the-heart' buyers.

The trend follower

Trend followers are celebrity spotters. They avidly read the celebrity gossip magazines and, if they see that someone they admire has just started a new trend – perhaps with a hairstyle, tattoo, beauty/health treatment, fashion accessory or clothes – they have to follow it. Their hope is that, if they emulate their idol, some of their 'stardust' may rub off on them. Plus they will be seen to be 'on trend' with the latest 'in thing'. The higher the profile their adored one has, the more the trend follower will want to replicate them. A prime example of this kind of idol is the Duchess of Cambridge. If she wears an outfit from a high-street retailer, it will instantly sell out, both in store and online.

These people are 'heart buyers', who may not necessarily think through their real reasons for making a purchase. For example, one serious downside of this behaviour has been the fallout from copying the 'handbag dog' accessory trend, i.e. carrying around a small dog in a handbag. First seen in the film *Legally Blonde* and then picked up by celebrities such as Paris Hilton, this treatment of small dogs as fashion accessories rather than as pets often results in the animals developing significant behavioural issues. Battersea Dogs Home has reported that they are increasingly being asked to rehome these disturbed small dogs.

The impulse buyer

Impulse buyers are easily influenced by other people's persuasiveness and by 'bargain' purchases, and they are often great fans of television shopping channels. Their emotional states often drive their spending habits. For example, if they feel sad, they will buy something to cheer themselves up. If they feel happy, they will splash out on a treat of some kind in order to celebrate. If they are out shopping with a friend who is buying, they join in because they tell themselves that it would be unsociable not to and, in any case, they deserve it (whatever 'it' happens to be).

Unfortunately, impulse buys are often not wise buys. The impulse buyer can easily end up with wardrobes full of clothes they never wear. Their 'spend, spend, spend' habit can even take them hurtling towards financial ruin. A famous example of this was the football pools winner Viv Nicholson, who won £152,319 in 1961 (£5 million in today's money), but who became penniless within a few years. These people are definitely 'from-the-heart' buyers.

The self-help junkie

On a permanent quest for personal growth, material success or spiritual enlightenment, the self-help junkie buys a huge number of books, ebooks, training programmes, CD sets and DVD sets on their chosen subject. They are often prepared to travel anywhere in the world to attend their favourite teacher or guru's seminars or retreats, where they hang on their every word. They consider their purchases to be investments, and it has to be said that some of these devotees do indeed utilize what they learn and go on to achieve all they desire in life. However, the majority of followers just accumulate a wealth of books that any library would be proud of, along with an extensive CD/DVD collection.

Until they feel that 'something' in their quest has made a difference to them, the self-help junkie will keep searching and buying because the answer has to be 'out there' somewhere; it's just a matter of time before they find it. They make intuitive, heart-based purchasing decisions in their search for fulfilment and happiness.

In order to influence others, especially in the context of selling them something, we must offer them something to which they will attribute value. This is why it's important to understand their personality type and what drives them to make purchasing decisions.

Personality and perceived value

You may have noticed that only the first two personality types described make 'head' decisions and that only one of those invests in purchases with the potential to increase in value. And yet 'value' is the common denominator for all six types. What converts a 'want' to a 'need' is its perceived value. Every one of the personality types listed has perceived a value of some kind in their potential purchases, and a 'need' has evolved that can only be satisfied by possessing it.

Let's revisit these personality types to understand the different values they attribute to their 'objects of desire'.

- **The gadget geek** is vulnerable to peer pressure and has an innate need to be 'leader of the pack'. This desire is so strong that it is programmed into their mental DNA and thus their purchasing decisions become logical, next-step actions. Possessing the most up-to-date, superior, shiny gadget has the value of fulfilling this non-negotiable need.
- **The connoisseur collector** is always focused on the financial value of a potential purchase and evaluates it in terms of future return on investment. He or she may invest in a Picasso that is not to their personal taste because they know that, whether it is hung on the wall or not, it is an asset that can only appreciate in value.
- **The memorabilia collector** has huge affection for their chosen theme. When they see a new 'desirable', especially if it is something they don't yet have in their collection, their heart starts racing and an 'inner smile' just takes them over. They take great care of their treasured objects and attach much value to their activity because of the happiness they gain from it. They find it hard to part with any of the objects they have collected, even when the size of their collection becomes excessive.
- **The trend follower** is searching for an identity. Lacking the courage to be original, they prefer to emulate others who they perceive to be setting new, desirable trends. Because their idols tend to be well known and publicly admired, the trend follower believes that they, too, will become popular if they dress the same way or do the same things. They have a strong need to feel admired and greatly value anything that might facilitate this.
- **The impulse buyer** readily responds to their emotions. He or she will 'invest' in something that will either change an undesirable emotional state or enhance an enjoyable one to make it last. For example, they are on holiday in Spain, having a marvellous time. On the last day they experience a burning desire to take something home

with them that will capture this sense of happiness. They browse the tourist shops and there it is – a straw donkey the size of a small child, wearing a sun hat. They have to have it! It's a challenge carrying it home on the plane but now it sits, in pride of place, in the hallway at home. It's in the way, of course, but every time our impulse buyer pats it on the head, happy memories of that holiday in Spain come flooding back.

- **The self-help junkie,** in search of personal fulfilment and meaning in life, attributes value to anything that appears to aid them in their quest. They see their chosen gurus as having successfully completed a journey upon which they are keen to embark. They are eager to learn and to replicate everything that their chosen one did along the way. If their guru is happy to impart this knowledge in a book, on a CD or DVD, or in person at a seminar, then the self-help junkie is a willing follower, valuing every morsel of advice they can glean.

The role of the champion

Another situation in which people place great value on their needs being met is during a time of crisis. People look for someone to become their 'champion', someone who will take control and lead them forward to happier times. Great value will be attributed to the person who fulfils this role and, in this position, he or she becomes extremely influential. Two examples of such champions are Winston Churchill and Bob Geldof.

The influence of Churchill

During the Second World War, Great Britain's 'champion' was Winston Churchill. An outstanding orator, his inspirational speeches provided a psychological boost to British morale exactly when it was needed. Two of his most memorable speeches – delivered in a tone of voice that resonated with unshakeable confidence and determination – were made during the dark days of 1940.

The first one came on 4 June, just hours after the evacuation of Dunkirk, in which 338,226 British and French soldiers, cut off by the German army, were rescued from the Dunkirk beaches by a hastily assembled fleet of 850 boats. Many of these boats were just small pleasure craft – the smallest was only 14 ft 7 in (4.45 m) long – but they all played an essential role in saving lives. The 'miracle of the little ships' has remained a prominent legend in Britain. Some of the surviving boats took part in the Queen's Diamond Jubilee river pageant in 2012, 72 years on from their finest hour.

The following is an extract from Churchill's post-Dunkirk speech:

> *We shall not flag or fail; we shall go on to the end. We shall fight in France; we shall fight on the seas and oceans. We shall fight with growing confidence and growing strength in the air. We shall defend our island whatever the cost may be. We shall fight on the beaches; we shall fight on the landing grounds. We shall fight in the fields and in the streets, we shall fight in the hills; we shall never surrender.*

Churchill referred to the outcome of the evacuation as a 'miracle' and the British press termed it a 'disaster turned into triumph'. To this day, the phrase 'Dunkirk spirit' is still used in Britain to describe people who pull together to overcome times of adversity.

Churchill made a second memorable speech on 20 August, when the crisis of the Battle of Britain was imminent. German air attacks were being directed against the RAF airfields in the south of England, and Churchill used the phrase 'so few' to describe the RAF fighter pilots:

> *The gratitude of every home in our Island, in our Empire, and indeed throughout the world, except in the abodes of the guilty, goes out to the British airmen who, undaunted by odds, unwearied in their constant challenge and mortal danger, are turning the tide of the world war by their prowess and by their devotion. Never in the field of human conflict was so much owed by so many to so few.*

The power of the pause

One technique that Churchill deployed in order to add impact to his speeches was the use of pauses. Read the following extract out loud, exactly as it is written:

'Never in the field of human conflict was so much owed by so many to so few.'

Now read it out loud again, pausing where there are dots, and notice the difference:

'Never ... in the field of human conflict ... was so much ... owed by so many ... to so few.'

Suddenly, it now has a deeper level of meaning, a gravitas that truly 'moved' people emotionally. Churchill knew about the power of the pause and he used it to great effect.

The influence of Bob Geldof

Another, more unlikely, champion emerged in 1984. On the evening of 23 October, rock singer Bob Geldof, like many thousands of others in Britain, was watching the 9 o'clock news on BBC television. Like thousands of others, he was appalled by a graphic report on the human suffering and huge loss of life occurring in Ethiopia as a result of drought, disease and famine.

In his view, '30 million people are dying; meanwhile, in Europe, we're spending tax to grow food we don't need, we spend more tax to store it and we pay further tax, most disgracefully, to destroy it.' He saw this as a crime; it made him angry and this galvanized him into action.

He *needed* to make a difference; the British public *wanted* to make a difference but didn't know how. Geldof had the answer. Within weeks, he had assembled a group of high-profile singers, and composed and recorded with them the Band Aid single, 'Do they know it's Christmas?' with the chorus of 'Feed the World'. It was released on 7 December, became the fastest-selling single ever and raised £8 million.

The following summer, Geldof initiated the satellite-linked UK and USA Live Aid concerts. By now he had support from the highest in the land, with Prince Charles and Princess Diana attending the Wembley concert alongside an audience of 72,000 people. TV pictures were beamed to over 1.5 billion people in 160 countries in the biggest broadcast ever known.

Between music sets, Geldof made frequent passionate appeals to viewers to 'Give us your money – there are people dying right now.' He shouted, he swore, and it worked. Across the UK, 200 phone lines were set up and manned to receive credit-card donations. Geldof personally took the call from the ruling family in Dubai when they made the biggest single donation of £1 million. In the USA, 22,000 pledges of money were received within five minutes of the Beach Boys taking to the stage in the simultaneous concert at JFK Stadium, Philadelphia.

Live Aid eventually raised a total of £40 million; in 1986 Bob Geldof was awarded an honorary knighthood. The success of Live Aid came about because Geldof had shown people a tangible way to make a difference to those who couldn't help themselves. Through our donations we could save lives and at the same time ease any feelings of guilt we may have been experiencing. And we placed *great value* on that.

You need to convey passion and conviction when you are aiming to influence others, and remember that part of what you are fulfilling is an emotional need.

Summary

In this lesson we have explored what influence is and how it manifests itself in our lives. We have looked at this in the context of how a 'want' can be transformed into a 'need' if sufficient value is added. This is apparent in our purchasing decisions, for a variety of different reasons, as demonstrated by the six 'buying personality' types.

We are also influenced and even inspired by 'champions' – people who step up into the leadership limelight just when we have an emotional need for someone to fill that role. Winston Churchill and Bob Geldof couldn't be more different and yet they both took on this role to great effect.

Value is thus the essential ingredient if we are thinking about influencing others. In order to influence others, we must offer them something to which they will attribute value. Whether it is a product or a well-reasoned argument that persuades people to do something or feel something, value is what makes the difference.

Fact-check (answers at the back)

1. What is influence?
a) Leaving a visible mark on someone ❑
b) The power someone has to affect other people's thinking or actions ❑
c) Preventing people doing what they want ❑
d) Forcing people to agree with you ❑

2. Which personality types buy 'from the head'?
a) The gadget geek and the connoisseur collector ❑
b) The memorabilia collector and the trend follower ❑
c) The impulse buyer and the self-help junkie ❑
d) The gadget geek and the trend follower ❑

3. How do people justify making a purchase?
a) By being influenced by other people's persuasiveness ❑
b) By copying other people's purchases ❑
c) They need to be bang up to date ❑
d) They convert their 'wants' into needs ❑

4. Which personality type focuses on particular themes?
a) The trend follower ❑
b) The memorabilia collector ❑
c) The gadget geek ❑
d) The impulse buyer ❑

5. What does every personality type need when buying?
a) To perceive a value in their potential purchases ❑
b) To follow their peer group rather than be leaders ❑
c) A potential return on their investment ❑
d) Admiration of their purchases by others ❑

6. Which personality type focuses on the potential return on their investment?
a) The self-help junkie ❑
b) The connoisseur collector ❑
c) The impulse buyer ❑
d) The trend follower ❑

7. Which personality type is in search of personal fulfilment?
a) The self-help junkie ❑
b) The connoisseur collector ❑
c) The impulse buyer ❑
d) The memorabilia collector ❑

8. What was Churchill's value as champion?
a) Supporting RAF fighter pilots ❑
b) Winning the Battle of Britain ❑
c) Inspiring people during a time of crisis ❑
d) Helping people to overcome adversity ❑

9. Prior to Live Aid, what was Bob Geldof famous for?
a) Being a TV chef ❑
b) Being a rock singer ❑
c) Making a difference ❑
d) Raising taxes to relieve suffering ❑

10. What was Bob Geldof's value as champion?

a) Enabling people to help save lives and at the same time ease any feelings of guilt ❑

b) Organizing a great rock concert ❑

c) Allowing credit-card donations ❑

d) Being awarded an honorary knighthood ❑

LESSON 2

Conveying the right image

Influencing effectively and powerfully is about more than just being a good speaker. We are most influenced by the type of person who 'walks their talk' – in other words, we look for congruence between the message and the person delivering it.

Even though Bob Geldof seemed initially an unlikely candidate for the role of global fundraiser and humanitarian, in his appearance, behaviour and communication style he remained true to his primary role of 'rock star'. We could label him 'the angry rock star, passionate about a good cause'. The pieces fitted together, we shared his mission and the whole package worked.

In this lesson we shall explore the consequences of being both totally congruent – when image, message and behaviour are all in alignment – and incongruent – where these elements are in conflict with each other. You will learn how and why people stereotype others, and how you can use this phenomenon to your advantage when influencing.

We shall also look at two individuals who have each in their own way been profoundly influential on a global scale. One overturned a stereotyped response and the other 'walked the talk'.

What is stereotyping?

As human beings, we have an innate desire to make sense of things. We need to know what's going on around us and how it affects us so that we can decide how to behave in response. This gives us a sense of comfort and the phrase 'comfort zone' is often used to describe this state of wellbeing. As part of this process, we like to draw rapid conclusions about our environment. For example, within four seconds of seeing someone for the first time, we start to make assumptions and judgements about them.

We may assume that at first glance we can tell the person's:

- age
- occupation
- financial worth
- lifestyle
- level of education
- ethnic origin
- marital status.

In addition, once the person starts to speak, we make further assumptions about their background, where they are from and even their level of intelligence, based on their accent or dialect, the type of vocabulary they use and their style of speech. At this point, our ego gets involved. We start to make comparisons between them and us, to determine how this person 'measures up'. Are they superior or inferior to us in some way? How should we behave towards them?

There is a danger here that we then act out an ego-driven behaviour based on false assumptions. If this happens, we may not be behaving in the most appropriate and best way possible, and in so doing we will not be able to influence effectively.

The positive purpose of stereotyping

However, this instant stereotyping can have a positive purpose, which is that it can protect us from danger. If we detect potential danger, our brain's fight-or-flight response allows us to take action against it. For example, imagine you are walking along a street at night and a figure steps out of the shadows in front of you. Your eyes scan him or her for signs of whether they are a friend or foe and, judging this stranger to have a 'menacing' appearance, your mind concludes that you could be in danger. This instantly triggers your fight-or-flight response, adrenaline is released into your body and you are now equipped either to stand your ground and defend yourself or to run away.

Because you have in your mind your own 'templates' of friend and foe, and you needed to make sense of the situation, you compared the appearance of the stranger before you to these images and found that he or she matched the 'foe template'. At that point, you stereotyped this person as some kind of troublemaker. You allowed yourself to be influenced by appearance and made an assumption that had at least a 50 per cent chance of being correct.

The first impression we form of someone tends to be a lasting one unless we receive some powerful and convincing evidence to the contrary. Moreover, our mind has a 'thinker' and a 'prover'. Whatever the thinker is thinking about, it is the prover's job to provide supporting evidence that says, 'Yes, you're right.' Once the thinker forms a first impression, the prover will only notice corroborative evidence; anything else will be dismissed as incorrect. This will continue until the thinker adopts a different viewpoint, but it usually takes something quite dramatic to bring about this 180° shift.

Overturning the stereotype: Susan Boyle

Susan Boyle is a Scottish singer who attracted worldwide public attention after appearing on the television show *Britain's Got Talent* in April 2009. Born in 1961 with a mild learning difficulty, Susan was bullied as a child and left school with few qualifications. However, her passion was singing and having taken part in, and won, several local amateur singing competitions, her mother urged her to enter the show in order to develop her confidence for singing in front of a large audience. Sadly, Susan's mother died before the audition took place and Susan nearly withdrew her application. However, her voice coach persuaded her to go ahead. Susan's performance on *BGT* was the first time she had sung in public since her mother's death.

When Susan walked out on the stage, a plain, slightly overweight, nearly 48-year-old, and said that her aspiration was to become a professional singer as successful as Elaine Paige, the audience laughed. They had stereotyped her in those first four seconds as delusional and decided that there was no way she could possibly be a talented singer. The judges clearly shared their scepticism, as this unlikely-looking candidate prepared to sing 'I dreamed a dream' from *Les Misérables.*

When Susan's clear, note-perfect mezzo-soprano voice filled the theatre, jaws dropped and eyes widened in astonishment at the clarity and beauty of her voice. The applause started just four seconds after Susan's first note and became a standing ovation that continued long after she'd finished singing, with the judges also on their feet. Judge Amanda Holden remarked on how the initially cynical attitude of the audience (and the judges) had been completely overturned by Susan's performance, calling it the 'biggest wake-up call ever'.

After that edition of *Britain's Got Talent* was televised, Susan appeared on the Oprah Winfrey show in the USA via satellite link. The final of that year's *BGT* commanded a record UK television audience of 17.3 million. Although favourite to win, Susan came second to dance troupe Diversity, but it didn't matter. She became a highly successful, internationally acclaimed professional singer, setting new records in both the UK and the USA for the fastest-selling album of a debut artist in decades.

Susan Boyle's story offers a profound example of how initial stereotyping based on appearance not only can be completely wrong but also *can* be overturned by overwhelming evidence to the contrary. However, she is the exception that proves the rule that 'You only get one chance to make a first impression'. It is far better to make the first impression the one you desire than to have to prove people wrong and force them to change their minds about you.

Tens of millions of people worldwide have already viewed the YouTube video of Susan Boyle's* Britain's Got Talent *audition. Watch it if you haven't already done so: it is an inspiring and even emotional experience to see it.

What is congruence?

An example of someone who very much 'walked her talk', whose appearance and behaviour were 100 per cent congruent with everything that she stood for – enabling her to exert her influence on a worldwide scale – was Anita Roddick, founder of The Body Shop. Although technically an international corporate executive, Anita never presented herself in a way that would have supported such a stereotype, for example dressing in a designer 'power suit' and high heels and carrying a smart leather briefcase. Such an image would have been at odds with The Body Shop 'brand' and seen as inauthentic.

The following case study about Anita Roddick shows the consequences of congruence. Anita believed that businesses have the power to do good in the world and The Body Shop mission statement reflects this sentiment and incorporates her own values, opening with the words, 'To dedicate our business to the pursuit of social and environmental change'. The Body Shop's mission had a global effect: it raised awareness of global issues, promoting third-world trade and discouraging the testing of products on animals. Because she lived her beliefs and values, both personally and in her business life, Anita Roddick will always remain synonymous with The Body Shop.

Walking the talk: Anita Roddick

Anita Roddick was born in a bomb shelter in 1942 in Littlehampton, Sussex, England, her Italian immigrant family having fled Naples just before the outbreak of the Second World War. Growing up in an English seaside town, Anita always felt she was a natural outsider, drawn to other outsiders and rebels such as her teenage idol James Dean. She also developed a strong sense of moral outrage at the age of ten when she read a book about the Holocaust.

Having trained as a teacher, she worked on a kibbutz in Israel, which led to an extended working trip around the world, during which she spent time in primitive farming and fishing communities, exposed to and learning about the body-care rituals of the women she encountered there. Influenced by her mother's wartime thriftiness of refilling, re-using and recycling, combined with a passion for environmental activism, Anita created a small range of body-care products and opened the first branch of The Body Shop in Brighton in 1976. Within six months, she had opened a second shop and eventually The Body Shop went global through the growth of a franchise network, serving some 77 million customers worldwide.

Anita always retained the appearance and demeanour of a 'wild child', her natural attractiveness the perfect advertisement for her beauty products. The issues she cared passionately about, such as social responsibility, respect for human rights, the environment, animal protection and community trade, became absorbed into The Body Shop's values. The company was at the forefront of using ingredients that had not been tested on animals and of actively trading with developing countries. For example, a moisturizing oil used in some of its products is extracted from Brazil nuts gathered sustainably by Amazonian Indian tribes.

During her lifetime, Anita was awarded many accolades, including the OBE in 1988 and the DBE in 2003, but perhaps one of the most significant and meaningful awards was presented to her in 1999 when she was made the 'Chief Wiper-Away of Ogoni Tears' for her involvement in the movement for the survival of the Ogoni people in Nigeria. Anita died in 2007, having fulfilled her promise to leave her estate to charities on moral grounds.

Presentation: the four-second rule

The way you present yourself sets the scene for how well you can influence others. The following table lists aspects of your appearance that people *will* notice within four seconds of meeting you. Although they might sound like common sense, neglecting any of these can result in the projection of a negative first impression, which can then undermine your ability to influence.

Aspect	Impression
Hair	Messy, unwashed hair or, worse, flakes of dandruff on your shoulders projects an extremely unprofessional image.
Nails	Bitten-down or dirty nails or chipped varnish indicate low personal standards.
Personal hygiene	A strong body odour makes it unpleasant to be around you. Ensure that you wash and use deodorant daily.
Perfume and aftershave	Use sparingly. An overwhelming 'vapour trail' can be almost as offensive as a strong body odour.
Breath	If you have been eating garlic or spicy food such as curry or drinking alcohol within the past 12 hours or so, your breath may still reflect this. Consider carrying mints and/or breath freshener with you at all times.

(*Continued*)

Aspect	Impression
Dress code	Always dress appropriately for your audience and take cultural norms into account. For men, this could mean a smart suit, collar and tie, and for women a skirt length on or below the knee and tights rather than bare legs. Whatever you are wearing, it must be clean and pressed. If you are a smoker, check for the smell of stale cigarette smoke on your clothes, as this will be particularly noticeable to non-smokers.
Shoes	Footwear must be clean and in good repair. Dirty, scuffed shoes with worn-down heels can let down the smartest outfit.
Tie	You may love the brightly coloured, cartoon-character tie your child gave you and it may reflect your quirky personality, but unless you know your audience really well, err on the side of formality and choose something more sober. Ensure that your tie has no marks or stains on it; because it is immediately below your face, it will always be noticed.
Neckline	Wearing a top with a low neckline is not acceptable in a business environment as it sends out the wrong message. Keep clothes like this for your personal life.
Frayed collars/ hanging threads/loose buttons	All indicate an attitude of neglect. Missing buttons, tears and holes are even worse. Make it a habit to carry out occasional wardrobe checks and repairs so that problems such as these can be avoided.
Jewellery	The principle of 'less is more' works well in the workplace, particularly for men. Wearing an excessive amount of jewellery distracts your audience from you and your message.
Make-up	As with jewellery and perfume, it is important not to wear too much. However, it should be noted that in a corporate environment, a woman wearing no make-up at all may be perceived as not professional enough. Cosmetics need to be well applied with subtlety so as to enhance rather than dramatically change the appearance of the wearer.
Handshake	A firm handshake, but not a bone-crusher, inspires confidence. A limp or damp handshake may be interpreted as a 'weak' personality trait.

Something as apparently insignificant as a stain on a tie or bitten-down fingernails can make the difference between your ability to be an effective influencer and a mediocre one. The little things really do make a big difference; take them seriously.

Consulting the professionals

To enhance aspects of your visual and vocal impact, which will in turn improve your ability to persuade and influence, think about consulting the following professionals.

Image consultant

An image consultant will carry out a colour and style analysis for you, enabling you to select clothes and colours that significantly enhance your appearance and improve your confidence levels. The intention is that you 'dress to impress', which will also strengthen your ability to influence others. A reputable image consultant can make all the difference to your 'visual charisma' and I cannot recommend this service highly enough.

Voice coach

If you feel that your voice lets you down in some way, consider consulting a voice coach. Many people in the public eye do this. Margaret Thatcher, in preparation for her bid to become leader of the Conservative Party, worked with such a coach, who enabled her to lower the pitch of her voice and slow down the speed of her vocal delivery. The result was that her voice gained an authority and gravitas that ultimately helped her to become the first female British prime minister.

Summary

In this lesson we discovered that, in order to influence and persuade effectively, it is essential to convey the right image. We explored the phenomenon of stereotyping and how this occurs naturally within the first four seconds of seeing someone for the first time. The example of Susan Boyle demonstrates this well, but it also shows that a negative stereotype *can* be turned around. However, it does require something extraordinary to make this happen.

For most situations it's important to make sure that you and your message are in complete alignment. Failure to do this results in an inauthentic impression of 'Do as I say', rather than 'Do as I do' and reduces your powers of persuasion. You may have noticed that politicians often fall foul of this principle!

To generate the most positive stereotype you can in those crucial first four seconds, you learned the importance of thinking about your personal presentation. The elements to consider may seem obvious, but they are easily overlooked. Consulting professionals can also help you to enhance your impact.

Fact-check (answers at the back)

1. What does 'congruent' mean?
   a) Your image, message and behaviour are out of alignment ❑
   b) You won't be stereotyped ❑
   c) Your image, message and behaviour are in alignment ❑
   d) We like people who look like us ❑

2. How quickly do we make assumptions about others?
   a) Within the first four seconds of seeing them ❑
   b) Within five minutes of seeing them ❑
   c) After we have talked to them at length ❑
   d) As soon as they start to speak ❑

3. What are stereotypes based on?
   a) Assumptions about others' financial worth ❑
   b) The attractiveness of someone ❑
   c) Comparisons with ourselves ❑
   d) What someone looks and sounds like ❑

4. What's the role of the ego when making assumptions?
   a) The ego never makes assumptions ❑
   b) Determining whether someone is superior or inferior to us ❑
   c) Making sure our assumptions are correct ❑
   d) Assumptions play no part in determining our behaviour ❑

5. What is the positive purpose of stereotyping?
   a) To protect us from potential danger ❑
   b) To release fight-or-flight hormones into the body ❑
   c) To make instant assumptions about others ❑
   d) To enhance our powers of persuasion ❑

6. How can we overcome initial stereotyping based on appearance?
   a) Through overwhelming evidence to the contrary ❑
   b) It's impossible ❑
   c) By ignoring our initial view ❑
   d) By forgetting what we first thought ❑

7. How does congruence enhance our ability to influence?
   a) By reflecting and incorporating our values into all our actions ❑
   b) By showing the world we mean business ❑
   c) By giving a good impression in a meeting ❑
   d) By making sure we dress smartly ❑

8. Why is the way you present yourself important?
   a) It helps us relax ❑
   b) It sets the scene for how well we can influence others ❑
   c) It keeps us one step ahead of the competition ❑
   d) It stops us feeling like a 'natural outsider' ❑

9. What's the best way to make a good impression?

a) Telling others to 'do as we say' rather than 'do as we do' ❑

b) Cultivating a 'lived-in' look to show we are 'hands-on' ❑

c) Paying attention to aspects of our appearance that people will notice ❑

d) Splashing out on perfume, aftershave or cologne ❑

10. What's a useful rule of presentation to remember?

a) Dress appropriately for your audience ❑

b) Scuffed shoes don't matter, as nobody will notice them ❑

c) Wear as much gold jewellery as possible, to impress others with your wealth ❑

d) A limp handshake is good, as it demonstrates your sensitive nature ❑

LESSON 3

Becoming a voice of authority

So far, we have looked at what influence is, the factors that affect it, both positively and negatively, and the importance of conveying the right image so that, when others construct a stereotype impression of you, it is exactly the one you intended. In this lesson we will explore how and why a voice of authority influences people.

The 'authority research' originally carried out by Stanley Milgram in the 1960s, and successfully replicated on television by Derren Brown in 2006, showed the extent to which people were willing to follow an authoritative voice, even to the point of them obeying that voice without question. Being aware of the conclusions from these experiments will enhance your ability to be authoritative, while remaining approachable and respected.

You'll also discover one of the reasons why Martin Luther King's famous 'I have a dream' speech had such a memorable impact and how you can adopt his tactic for yourself when making a presentation. You will also learn a technique for sounding assertive, reasonable and in control in even the most confrontational situations, as well as some other proven strategies for becoming a confident, effective and influential figure of authority.

Who are your authority figures?

Let's start by examining examples of authority figures. Think back to your childhood and specifically to the people who represented figures of authority to you. These are the people who impressed and inspired you, people you admired and respected. If one of these people asked you to do something, you would have done it willingly and without question. You listened to their advice and took it on board. They may have been your parents or other family members, a teacher, a friend or someone else in your peer group, a neighbour or some other member of your community.

Identify three of these authority figures and write down their names in a table like the one below. Then, for each one, define exactly what characteristic(s) it was about them that generated your respect and prompted you to call them to mind.

Name	Characteristic(s)
1	
2	
3	

Now repeat the exercise, this time identifying the authority figures you feel you have in your life now. Choose three people whom you did not select before, and include any public figures who fulfil the criteria for you, even if you have never met them. The following are typically some of the characteristics that you may have identified:

Good listener
Very understanding
Showed compassion and empathy
Championed my cause
Took a genuine interest in me
Always had time for me, even when busy
Believed in me and my ideas
Led by example
Gave support and encouragement
Brave, courageous
Light-hearted, always positive and smiling
Never made unreasonable or unfair demands
Generous spirit
Decisive
Knowledgeable and competent

Reassuring
Optimistic in the face of uncertainty
An achiever, but never arrogant about it
Happy to share their ideas/ solutions with me
Prepared to step up and lead when someone was needed
Took complete responsibility for him/herself and his/her actions
Always embraced a challenge
Constantly strove to be their 'best self' and to make a difference to others
Good problem solver with innovative ideas

You may have identified some additional ones. However, the common theme here is that all of these are qualities we tend to admire and respect so, if we attribute any of them to another person, we are more likely to accept them as a figure of authority, deserving our respect and co-operation.

In identifying significant authority figures from your childhood, you were recalling people who were important to you when you were at an impressionable age. You may have found that, when you then identified more recent authority figures, the characteristics you sought in them were different from the childhood ones.

Now take some time to review the list above and the characteristics you identified in this exercise. How many of these attributes do *you* have? The more of these that you possess, the easier it will be for you to become a figure of authority.

Select a characteristic from the list that you feel you don't currently have and set yourself an action plan to develop it.

The Milgram experiments

During the early 1960s the Yale University social psychologist Stanley Milgram conducted some experiments. His intention was to measure the willingness of participants to obey an authority figure – one who would instruct them to perform actions that conflicted with their personal conscience and deepest moral beliefs.

The experiment involved three roles:

- The experimenter – this was an authoritative role of 'experimental scientist'
- The teacher – this role was fulfilled by a volunteer, intended to obey the orders of the experimenter
- The learner – this was a role fulfilled by an actor who pretended to be another volunteer, and who would be the recipient of the actions carried out by the teacher

Although the volunteer and the actor drew slips of paper to determine their roles, both slips would say 'teacher' and the actor would always claim that his slip read 'learner'. They were then separated into different rooms where they could communicate but not see each other. In some instances, the learner would make a point of mentioning to the teacher that he had a heart condition.

The teacher was then told that he/she would be teaching a list of word pairs to the learner. Having read through the entire list to the learner, the teacher would then read the first word of each pair together with a list of four possible answers. The learner would press a button to indicate his response. If the answer was correct, the teacher would read the next word pair. However, if the answer was incorrect, the teacher would administer an electric shock to the learner, with the voltage increasing in 15-volt increments for each wrong answer. Before commencing, the teacher was given a mild electric shock as a sample of the initial shock they would be administering to the learner.

In fact, the learner in the next room received no electric shocks whatsoever. The actor playing this role would deliberately get some answers wrong and then react to the 'shock' administered by the teacher by crying out, apparently in pain. With each increase in voltage, the actor would also ramp up his performance so that it would sound as if he was in significant distress, at times even begging for the exercise to stop.

Meanwhile, the teacher was being instructed by the experimenter – as the voice of authority – to continue administering the increasingly powerful 'shocks' despite the apparent cries of pain from the learner. Throughout the experiment, the volunteer 'teachers' displayed varying degrees of tension and stress. Every one of them at some point paused and questioned the experiment but, nevertheless, more than 60 per cent of them continued up to the point where they were inflicting 'fatal voltages'.

Milgram and obedience to authority

The conclusions drawn from the Milgram experiments were as follows:

1 Somebody who has neither the ability nor the expertise to make decisions, especially in a crisis, will leave decision making to someone they consider to be more authoritative.
2 If a person comes to view themselves as the instrument for carrying out another person's wishes, they will no longer see themselves as responsible for their actions.
3 When experts tell people something is all right, they think it probably is, even if it does not seem to be.

Derren Brown's *The Heist*

In 2006, as part of a UK Channel 4 TV special called *The Heist*, Derren Brown re-enacted the Milgram experiments as part of a selection process to determine which of his volunteers would be prepared to stage an armed robbery, if instructed to do so. The results were almost identical to those of the original experiments, with over 50 per cent of participants continuing to administer 'shocks' up to the fatal voltage of 450V. From his final selection of four candidates, three did in fact carry out an 'armed' robbery of a security van, albeit with toy guns.

After filming, all four participants were 'deprogrammed' of any temporary criminal inclinations, spending time with Brown and an independent psychologist. *The Heist* faced some controversy after it was aired, but the four final participants reported that they were all pleased with the programme and, indeed, they are shown stating that it was a positive experience. A 2011 viewer poll revealed that *The Heist* was the viewers' favourite of all of Derren Brown's specials.

Similarly, 84 per cent of Milgram's participants surveyed after his experiments said that they had been 'glad' or 'very glad' to have taken part. Many of them wrote to Milgram later to express their thanks and some offered further assistance or asked to join his staff.

Authority and leadership

While it is unlikely that you would want to influence people to administer electric shocks to others or carry out an armed robbery, the following learning points are also relevant to a leadership or other influential role in a business environment:

1. If people are in a situation of uncertainty, they not only look to be led but *like* to be led and to be told what to do.
2. The views of someone who appears to be knowledgeable, confident, assured and an expert in their field are unlikely to be challenged.
3. Because of the previous two learning points, it is vital that the person fulfilling the role of authority figure conducts him- or herself with the utmost personal integrity.

Influencing with the 'power of three'

Although this book is not primarily about selling techniques or presentation skills, it is worth examining a principle that works effectively as a 'convincer' and is therefore a good tactic to use in a situation where you need to be influential.

Research has shown that people need repetition in order to feel 'convinced'. Further, it has been found that the 'magic' number of repetitions is three. In a sales context, this is often used as a closing technique where the sales person will ask the potential customer three questions, to which the answers will most likely be yes. The fourth question will then be the 'closing-the-deal' question and, because the customer has just replied positively three times, there is a strong chance that they will say yes again.

The power of three in action

Q1. 'So have I covered everything you need to know about this product?'

A. 'Yes.'

Q2. 'And you're happy with our free delivery service?'

A. 'Yes.'

Q3. 'And it's this particular model that you're interested in, isn't it?'

A. 'Yes.'

Q4. 'Good. So shall we process the paperwork and get it all sorted for you now?'

A. 'Yes.'

The same principle, of the power of three, also works well as a convincer when we are making a presentation. For example, a commonly used presentation structure is:

1 Tell them what you're going to tell them (introduction).
2 Tell them (content).
3 Tell them what you've told them (conclusion).

This structure means that your content is, in fact, delivered three times and thus gains more impact and becomes more memorable. There are many ways of using the power of three in a presentation or speech.

Martin Luther King and the power of three

An American Baptist minister, Martin Luther King Jr was best known for his role as a leader in the African-American civil rights movement. An advocate of non-violent civil disobedience, in 1964 he received the Nobel Peace Prize for combating racial inequality through non-violence and, over the next few years, until his assassination in 1968, he was also an activist in the fight against poverty and the Vietnam War.

In 1963, during a march on Washington, he established a reputation as one of the greatest orators in American history when he delivered his 'I have a dream' speech. Although it was just one of many speeches he delivered during his career, this is the one that people tend to remember him for, and the power of three played a very important part in it.

King not only used the power of three with the phrase 'I have a dream' but he also used it *to* the power of three – in other words, three times three times, in a total of nine iterations. The following is an extract from that speech with the key phrase shown in bold a total of nine times:

And so even though we face the difficulties of today and tomorrow, ***I*** *still* ***have a dream.*** *It is a dream deeply rooted in the American dream.*

I have a dream *that one day this nation will rise up and live out the true meaning of its creed, 'We hold these truths to be self-evident, that all men are created equal.'*

I have a dream *that one day on the red hills of Georgia, the sons of former slaves and the sons of former slave owners will be able to sit down together at the table of brotherhood.*

I have a dream *that one day even the state of Mississippi, a state sweltering with the heat of injustice, sweltering with the heat of oppression, will be transformed into an oasis of freedom and justice.*

I have a dream *that my four little children will one day live in a nation where they will not be judged by the colour of their skin but by the content of their character.*

I have a dream *today!*

I have a dream *that one day, down in Alabama, with its vicious racists, with its governor having his lips dripping with the words of 'interposition' and 'nullification' – one day right there in Alabama, little black boys and black girls will be able to join hands with little white boys and white girls as sisters and brothers.*

I have a dream *today!*

I have a dream *that one day every valley shall be exalted and every hill and mountain shall be made low, the rough places will be made plain, and the crooked places will be made* *straight; 'and the glory of the Lord shall be revealed and all flesh shall see it together.'*

This is our hope, and this is the faith that I go back to the South with.

After using the phrase for the first time, King repeated it *at the beginning* of each of the next eight statements, which was another good tactic for making it memorable and for positioning himself as a voice of authority.

Authority and tone of voice

In order to project a voice of authority, it is important that you consistently speak with a confident, firm (but not arrogant) tone. As already mentioned, Margaret Thatcher worked with a voice coach to lower her voice pitch and slow down her pace of speaking in order to give gravitas and authority to her voice. King George VI famously worked with Australian speech therapist Lionel Logue in order to overcome a stammer that was proving to be a major vocal impediment for his many public-speaking duties. (The story is captured in the film *The King's Speech*, which won Colin Firth an Oscar for his excellent portrayal of the king.)

Bad habits

When presenting, beware of the following (very common) habits that can undermine your voice of authority:

- Making very little eye contact with your audience
- Saying 'um' or 'err' a lot
- Speaking too quietly for people at the back to be able to hear you
- Rocking on your feet
- Turning your back to your audience to read from the PowerPoint slide displayed behind you
- Repeatedly clicking the top of a ballpoint pen
- Fiddling with cufflinks

- Fiddling with jewellery
- Repeatedly scratching the top of your head
- Clapping your hands together at the end of every sentence
- Hands in pockets
- Twiddling long hair around a finger

The best way to ensure that you are not guilty of any of these is to rehearse your presentation several times beforehand, and finally in front of someone who will give you honest feedback and/or in front of a camera so that you can critique yourself.

Sounding firm, fair and assertive

Maintaining a voice of authority when faced with an aggressive person or some other confrontational situation can be a challenge. However, the following structure, known as the **assertive sentence**, works extremely well. The results you get will greatly increase your confidence and generate a perception of you as someone who sounds like a voice of authority, to be respected. The assertive sentence is a valuable 'tool' to have in your mental toolbox, to use whenever an opportunity arises.

The assertive sentence has four parts, as follows:

1. **Acknowledge the other person's situation** – this demonstrates that you have listened to them and that you understand their position.
2. **Next, say 'However...'** – never use the word 'but', which will set up a barrier to what you are going to say next.
3. **State your position** – this might be quite different from theirs and needs to be out in the open.
4. **Suggest a mutually acceptable outcome** – you are looking for a workable compromise, a 'win/win' that will accommodate both their needs and yours.

An example of this is:

> *'I appreciate that you currently have a very high workload; however, your input at today's meeting is vital so that important decisions can be made, and therefore I'd be grateful if you could attend for the first 20 minutes to provide us with your data.'*

The end result always sounds very reasonable and, because the other person's situation has been acknowledged right at the beginning of the sentence, it is hard for them to refuse to co-operate. However, if you don't get the desired result the first time, and particularly if the other person says, 'Yes, but...' and puts forward another line of argument, then run through it again, this time using their new situation at the beginning.

Summary

In this lesson we explored how you can become a 'voice of authority' by looking at the characteristics of someone acknowledged as an authority figure.

The research by Stanley Milgram, later replicated by Derren Brown, proves that, in certain circumstances, people will do whatever they are told to do if they believe that the request is initiated by someone who is knowledgeable and in a position of authority. If you relate this to the business environment, you may observe that effective leaders tend to be those who are perceived as having expertise combined with confidence.

The power of three is a 'convincer strategy' that works well in a variety of situations, including that of making an influential presentation. The analysis of Martin Luther King's famous 'I have a dream' speech shows that that key phrase was used three times multiplied by another three times, for maximum effect.

You also learned about the importance of tone of voice, the bad habits to avoid and a technique for sounding firm, fair and assertive.

Fact-check (answers at the back)

1. What's an 'authority figure'?
a) Someone older than you are ❑
b) Someone not generally respected ❑
c) Someone who impresses and inspires others ❑
d) Someone who, if they asked you to do something, you would refuse ❑

2. What is a key skill of an authority figure?
a) The ability to listen ❑
b) Seeming to be too busy to have time for others ❑
c) The ability to sound like an expert ❑
d) The ability to enforce obedience ❑

3. What characterizes authority figures?
a) Arrogance ❑
b) A habit of making unreasonable demands on others ❑
c) A willingness to keep secrets ❑
d) The ability to embrace a challenge ❑

4. What were the Milgram experiments designed to measure?
a) Obedience to an authority figure ❑
b) Disobedience to a teacher ❑
c) How people learn ❑
d) How people react to electric shocks ❑

5. What roles did participants play in the Milgram experiments?
a) Experimenter, teacher and learner ❑
b) Questioner, teacher, onlooker ❑
c) Interrogator, victim, onlooker ❑
d) Evaluator, learner, convincer ❑

6. What were the conclusions of the Milgram experiments?
a) People will let an authority figure make decisions for them ❑
b) If people see themselves as the instrument for carrying out another person's wishes, they won't feel responsible for their actions ❑
c) People learn that, when experts tell them something is all right, it probably is, even if it does not seem so ❑
d) All of the above ❑

7. How many 'teachers' in the Milgram experiment continued to increase the voltage up to fatal levels?
a) Fewer than 20 per cent ❑
b) 35 per cent ❑
c) More than 60 per cent ❑
d) 100 per cent ❑

8. What was the purpose of *The Heist* TV special?
a) To stage an armed robbery of a bank ❑
b) To show that people can be influenced to behave out of character ❑
c) To show people receiving electric shocks ❑
d) To show that people like to be told what to do ❑

9. What is an effective method of convincing people of something?

a) Clapping the hands together loudly ❑

b) To use the 'power of three' technique ❑

c) Mentioning it once is enough ❑

d) To speak in a soft tone of voice ❑

10. What's the best way to project a voice of authority during a confrontation?

a) To speak quietly and hesitantly ❑

b) To use the assertive sentence technique ❑

c) To avoid making eye contact in case they turn hostile ❑

d) Keeping your hands in your pockets ❑

LESSON 4

Speaking the language of influence

The best influencers are superb communicators – this is the *key* skill that will deliver the best results for you.

Whether you're communicating with others face to face, over the telephone or in writing, you need to be clear, positive and persuasive. Your message does not have to be verbal: even the way you dress delivers a message about you that may enhance or damage your ability to influence others.

In this lesson we will explore how to improve your communication using proven, effective techniques. You will learn about rapport, why it's essential to have it in order to influence others, and how to build it effortlessly and rapidly. You will understand what makes everyone unique, and why it's so important to have a flexible communication style in order to influence the maximum number of people.

You will also learn how to calm down an angry person easily and assertively, without taking on board their emotional state. You will discover the language to use and the actions to take to get people on board with your way of thinking. You will even learn how to 'read' people's eye movements and understand what they *really* mean.

There is only one version of you

Each one of us is as individual as a fingerprint. Although we might be similar to others, there will always be differences that contribute to our uniqueness. The way we make sense of the world around us – and how we think, feel and behave as a result of that – has an effect on how we communicate with others and how we like others to communicate with us. By understanding how this process works, you can start to develop flexibility in your communication style, which will enable you to become far more persuasive.

The following diagram represents the 'core model' of neuro-linguistic programming (NLP) and illustrates how we take in information from around us (external events), pass it through our own individual set of 'filters', make sense of it, react to it emotionally and physically, and finally behave in a way that feels appropriate to us.

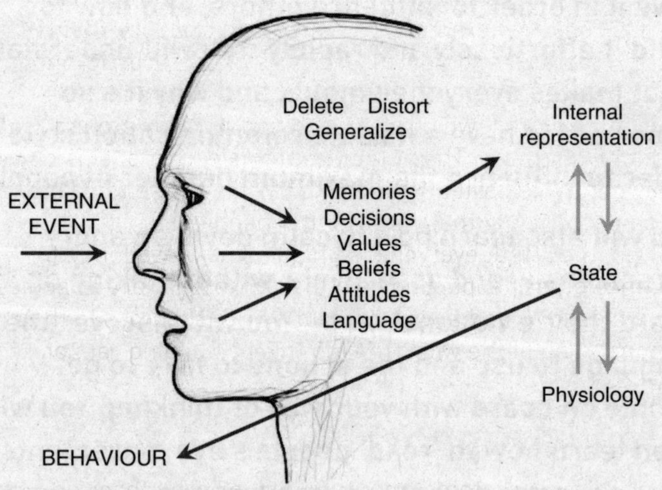

The NLP model of what we do with external information

We take in what is going on around us through our five senses. However, if we tried to process all this information, it would be more than our conscious mind, with its limited capacity, could handle. By contrast, the unconscious mind has a virtually unlimited capacity: it contains thoughts, memories and desires as well as automatic skills that are under the surface of our conscious awareness but which still have a great impact on our behaviour.

Filters and our 'map of the world'

To protect our conscious mind from overload, we all have a set of 'filters', made up of such things as memories, decisions, values, beliefs, attitudes, language and a lot more. We create and amend these filters as we progress through life, based on our ongoing experiences. Because everyone's experiences of life are different, everyone's set of filters is unique to them.

The role of the filters is to delete, distort or generalize information coming in, in order to make sense of it. The information then becomes an 'internal representation' of what is going on outside us – in other words, it becomes a thought. Attached to the thought is a state of mind, or emotion, so the thought could, for example, be happy, sad or angry. Aligned to the emotional state of mind is the physiology, or body language.

As a result of this whole process, we create an internal 'map of the world', which we use to find our way around the 'territory' out there. The output from this core model is our behaviour, which will always make perfect sense to us but may not be perceived in that way by other people.

Given, then, that everyone is unique, it is a challenge to influence other people and gain their co-operation. To achieve this, we need to find a way to 'build a bridge' across to their personal map of the world. We do this by building rapport.

What is rapport?

The word rapport stems from the French verb *rapporter,* which literally means to carry something back. In 'building our bridge' across to someone else, they connect with us and a feeling of mutual understanding flows right back. If you experience resistance or negativity in someone you wish to influence, this may indicate that rapport is missing.

Rapport builds naturally and can often be witnessed when the body language of two people who are getting on well together becomes 'matched' or 'mirrored'. Matching means that their body language is identical – for example, each person has their right leg crossed over their left and is leaning to their left. Mirroring means that one person is the mirror image of the other, so if one of them has their right leg crossed over their left and is leaning to their left, the other person will have their left leg crossed over their right and be leaning to their right. You are more likely to be *matched* with someone you are sitting or standing next to and *mirrored* with someone opposite you. Both are external indicators that rapport has been built.

This natural matching and mirroring process is also referred to as 'entrainment'.

Entrainment

A Dutch scientist named Christian Huygens discovered the phenomenon of entrainment in about 1665. Huygens had a room with a number of pendulum-driven clocks in it, and he observed that, over time, the pendulums of all the clocks fell into synchronization with each other. Even if he deliberately started them swinging at different times, he would inevitably return to find they had all become synchronized. He named this synchronization tendency 'entrainment'.

Building rapport

It is, of course, possible to speed up this process of rapport building through entrainment by deliberately matching or mirroring the other person. If you choose to do this, subtlety is essential because, if what you are doing is too obvious, it may cause offence.

The following pie chart shows the three elements of communication – physiology (body language), tone of voice and words – and their relative proportions. Much research has been conducted on these figures, principally by Albert Mehrabian, Professor Emeritus of Psychology at UCLA.

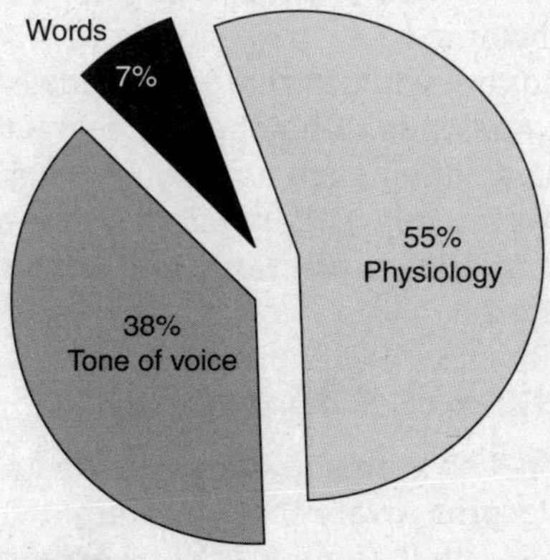

Segments of communication

The largest slice of the pie is physiology, or body language, at 55 per cent. Even if you are not speaking, your body language 'speaks' for you. However, on the telephone, you have lost this element because your body language cannot be seen. However, a smile can be heard: if you change the shape of your mouth into a smile, your voice will sound different. It will sound happier and more positive, so it's always a good idea to answer the phone with a smile on your face.

Let's explore how you can utilize each of these three elements to build rapport.

Physiology – the 55 per cent

Start by matching or mirroring the other person's posture, gestures and movements. Be careful to avoid mimicry. For example, if someone is sitting opposite you and they suddenly cross their legs, lean forward, put one elbow on the table and rest their chin on their hand, do not immediately do the same thing. This would be too obvious and could well cause offence.

Instead, make gradual movements of your own until you have created a similarity to their body language.

Matching another person's breathing rate is a far more subtle and yet powerful way to build rapport. Watch for the slight rise and fall of their shoulders and adjust your breathing into the same rhythm.

The final thing that you can match on body language is your blink rate. Again, don't be obvious, and if the other person has an eye defect such as a squint, don't hurt their feelings by mirroring this. Otherwise this is another very effective way of creating a similarity and building rapport at an unconscious level.

Tone of voice – the 38 per cent

Have you ever spoken with someone who had a strong accent or dialect and become aware that you were unintentionally starting to speak in that same accent or dialect? This is a guaranteed way of offending through mimicry, caused by your unconscious mind's desire to create a similarity and build rapport. Although this can happen when you are speaking face to face, it is more likely to happen during a telephone conversation, when physiology plays very little part and tone of voice becomes approximately 80 per cent of the communication.

Instead, you can safely match the following characteristics of the other person's voice:

- volume
- speed
- tone
- pitch
- energy
- intonation
- phrasing

Imagine for a moment that you have an angry person in front of you. What has happened to their voice? It has probably speeded up, got louder and become higher pitched. Perhaps you've been in this situation and you chose to stay really calm, but the other person, instead of calming down, got even angrier. The reason for this is that rapport was lacking; the gap between you was too wide for you to be able to be a calming influence on them. The other person's unconscious mind was telling him or her that, because you were so different from them, you just didn't understand the gravity of the situation and so they would have to 'ramp up' their own behaviour in order to make their point more clearly.

In this scenario, you can use a technique called *pacing and leading*. If you listen to the vocal characteristics of this angry person and reply using those same characteristics, you are expressing empathy and building a bridge across to their map of the world. This is called *pacing*. After a short time of doing this, start to slow down your voice, turn down the volume and lower the pitch. If sufficient rapport has been built, the other person will now start to follow you and calm down. You are now *leading*. This is a very effective strategy and, because the other person is responding at an unconscious level, it will feel completely natural to them and not manipulative at all.

Words – the 7 per cent

Words form the smallest element of communication. If ever you have spent many hours writing a speech or a presentation, you will be pleased to know that this constituted just 7 per cent of your total message. The other 93 per cent was conveyed in how you stood up and delivered it! Over the telephone, words play a greater part in rapport building, increasing in value to about 20 per cent.

In order to match someone else on their vocabulary, listen for the following:

- **Key words** – these are either individual words or short phrases that we like and use a lot. They vary from individual to individual, depending on their preferences, and may include words such as:
  - basically
  - actually
  - cool

- like
- you know
- OK
- at the end of the day
- the bottom line is...

If you detect that someone is using a particular word or short phrase repeatedly, then you are hearing their key words. When you respond to them, incorporate those same words into your reply, and you are then 'speaking their language'. A word of caution – do not reflect back their key words in every sentence you speak as it will be too obvious that this is what you are doing.

- **VHF words** – when we speak, we tend to use words that fit into our preferred 'channel' of communication. These can be:
  - **visual**
    'I see what you mean', 'Looks good to me', 'Show me more'
  - **hearing**
    'I hear what you're saying', 'That rings a bell', 'Sounds familiar'
  - **feeling**
    'I want to get a grip on this idea', 'I'm going with my gut feeling', 'That really touched me', etc.

If you can hear someone using vocabulary that falls predominantly into one of these three channels, then adjust your language so that you are using the same type of words. When you do this, you have 'tuned into their wavelength' and can begin to 'speak their language'.

What's your preference?

Because we naturally communicate in the channel that is our predominant one, you may not be aware of whether your preference is visual, hearing or feeling. Complete the following questionnaire by reading each question in turn and circling the answer a, b or c that is most appropriate for you.

Question	Answer
1 What would make you think that someone might be lying to you?	a) The way they look – or avoid looking – at you b) Their tone of voice c) A feeling you get about their sincerity
2 How do you know that you have had a good day at work?	b) A productive meeting or good news over the telephone a) A clear desk or a 'to do' list with everything ticked off c) An inner glow, a smile and a feeling of deep satisfaction
3 What kind of activity do you prefer on holiday?	c) Lazing on a sun-drenched beach, swimming to cool off b) Attending a concert or a lecture on local culture and history a) Seeing the sights and local colour, visiting a museum or art gallery
4 Which of the following groups of hobbies/ interests appeals most to you?	a) Cinema, photography, art, interior design c) Sport, sculpture, cookery, gardening b) Playing a musical instrument, listening to music or an audio book, singing.
5 What types of television programme do you prefer to watch?	c) Wildlife and animals a) An artist at work b) Musical concert
6 Which of the following would you prefer as a 'special' treat?	b) A personal dedication on the radio by a celebrity you admire a) A weekend break away somewhere you have never visited before c) Your favourite meal with good wine and good company
7 Which would be the best way for you to unwind at the end of a hard day?	a) Gazing at something relaxing such as a candle flame c) An aromatherapy massage b) Talking to a friend
8 If you want to thank or reward someone for doing you a favour, what would you do?	b) Telephone them to tell them how grateful you are c) Give them a bottle of their favourite drink/bottle of perfume a) Write them a thank-you note

(*Continued*)

Question	Answer
9 Which of the following groups of careers most appeals?	a) An artist or designer in television b) Lecturer, telesales or professional speaker c) Gardener, nurse or counsellor
10 Which accessories do you like to have in your home?	b) Wind chimes, background music, ticking clock a) Lots of pictures, accented lighting, a focal point, e.g. a fireplace c) Pot-pourri, soft cushions, comfortable, squashy chairs
11 Which type of magazine would you be most likely to pick up and read?	c) Home decorating, sports or creative crafts b) Music or current affairs a) Art, photography or fashion
12 How would you discipline a naughty child?	a) With a severe look or frown c) With punishment by deprivation, e.g. no pocket money b) By shouting or using a stern tone of voice

Add up your scores by letter and make a note of them.

a) .... (visual)
b) .... (hearing)
c) .... (feeling)

Your preferred 'channel' is the one with your highest score.

The VHF types

The following are descriptions of the three types. Notice whether the description of your preferred 'channel' is a good match for you.

- **Visual**
  Typically, people who are in a visual mode stand or sit with their heads erect and their eyes up and will be breathing from the top of their lungs. They often sit forward in their chair or on the edge of the chair. They tend to be quite organized, neat, well groomed and orderly. They are appearance-oriented, and may sometimes be quieter than other people. They are generally good spellers, memorize

by seeing pictures and are not easily distracted by noise. They may have trouble remembering verbal instructions and are bored by long verbal explanations because their mind tends to wander. They would rather read than be read to and, ideally, like to have information presented to them using pictures, charts and diagrams.

A visual person will be interested in how someone looks at them, and will notice details of others' appearance such as their dress style. They will tend to use visual imagery in phrases like 'See you later', 'Looking good', 'In my mind's eye', 'I get the picture', etc.

- **Hearing**

Someone who has a 'hearing' preference will move their eyes sideways and may tilt their head to one side when they are listening. They breathe from the middle of the chest. They often move their lips when they are mentally saying words and may even talk to themselves when thinking something through. They are easily distracted by noise but can generally repeat things back to you easily. They may find spoken language easier than maths and writing. They like music and learn by listening; they memorize by using steps, procedures and sequences.

A 'hearing' person is often interested in being told how they're doing and is more likely to notice tone of voice and other vocal characteristics. They tend to use hearing imagery in words and phrases like 'Tell me more', 'That rings a bell', 'Sounds familiar', etc.

- **Feeling**

There are two types of 'feeling' people. The first type has a posture that tends to slump over and they may move and talk slowly. They are laid back, with a calm demeanour, and fond of relaxing. The second type is more active and 'talks with their hands', i.e. they gesticulate when speaking and may fidget when sitting still. Both types will typically access their feelings and emotions to 'get a feel' for what they're doing, so they may be naturally intuitive.

Feeling people can be quite tactile and they like to learn by doing – the 'hands-on' approach. These people will really notice a limp handshake and be thoroughly unimpressed by it! They use feeling words and phrases like 'I've got a gut feeling', 'Get in touch', 'I'm going with my instincts', 'Let's make contact', etc.

Eye movements and thinking styles

Imagine that you're having a face-to-face conversation with someone. You're listening for the VHF words but the language seems neutral. There is another way of telling whether someone is thinking in pictures, sounds or feelings and that is by the way their eyes move when they are thinking of what they are going to say next or when they are processing the answer to a question.

Carry out the following exercise with the participation of someone else. You will see that there are a series of questions, five for 'A' and five for 'B'. Take it in turns to ask each other the questions, one of you as 'A' and the other as 'B'. Use a grid for each question like the one shown below and, for each one, position your pen or pencil in the middle of the grid and trace the other person's eye movements on the grid as they mentally process the answer to that question. Draw exactly what you see. If their eyes move upwards and to the right, draw that, even though this would be to their left. The eyes may move to several different places before the answer has been processed and this is fine – just track every movement you observe on to the grid.

Questions for 'A'

1 What does your favourite actor sound like?
2 What would a pink giraffe look like if it were wearing sunglasses and open-toed sandals?
3 Can you spell your full name backwards?
4 What was the front-page headline in your newspaper yesterday?
5 What would the national anthem sound like if it were sung backwards, under water?

Questions for 'B'

1 What would a whale singing 'Happy birthday to you' sound like?
2 How many doors are there in your home?
3 Who was the first person you spoke to on the telephone yesterday?
4 What clothes were you wearing last Saturday?
5 How much is 1,296 divided by 4?

When we are thinking about what we are going to say next, or we are processing the answer to a question, our eyes move in particular directions, depending on whether we are mentally processing in pictures, sounds or feelings.

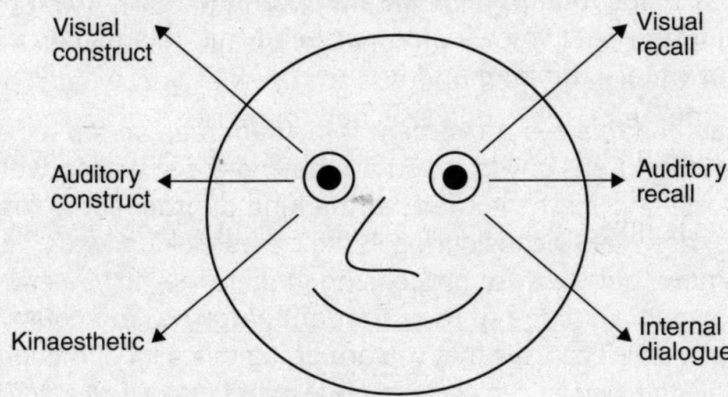

How people think – eye-accessing cues

V: visual thinkers

If the eyes go up, we are visualizing:

- Up and to our right (left if you are observing someone else's eyes) means that we are visually constructing an image of something we haven't seen before.

- Up and to our left (right if you are observing someone else) means that we are visually recalling something that we have seen before.
- We are also visually processing if our eyes are looking straight ahead into the distance, or if they are closed, as if we are getting images on the backs of our eyelids.

H: hearing thinkers

- If our eyes move sideways and to our right (left in someone you are observing), we are imagining what something could sound like that we haven't heard before.
- If our eyes move sideways and to our left (right in someone you are observing), then we are remembering what something sounds like that we have heard before.

F: feeling thinkers

- If our eyes move down and to our right (left in someone you are observing), then we are processing in feelings, or kinaesthetically. These could be emotions or we could be imagining the physical feel of touching something.
- If our eyes move down and to our left (right in someone you are observing), then we are listening to our internal dialogue – that voice inside our head that lets us know what we are thinking and feeling.

You can use this eye movement information as an aid to influencing. Let's say that you are having a discussion with someone and you have made some kind of proposal to them. As they are silently considering it, their eyes look upwards. You now know that they are processing in pictures, so you could match your language to their thought patterns. You could, for example, say, 'I can *see* that you are giving this a lot of thought. Is there anything else I can *show* you that might make it *clearer*?'

You cannot* not *communicate. Even if you are not speaking, your body language and overall appearance will speak for you. Make sure the message that you're sending out is the one you want to convey.

Rapport in writing

If you are writing to someone and you don't know their preferred VHF channel, or if you are writing something that will be read by many people – so that there will be a mix of all three channels – then balance the number of visual, hearing and feeling words you use. This will ensure that at least a third of your text will be 'speaking their language'. For example, 'We love to keep *in touch* with our customers, to *show* them that we are really interested in *hearing* how they are getting on.'

One author who does this very effectively and successfully is J. K. Rowling. If you open any of her Harry Potter books anywhere, you will see that she has skilfully balanced the visual, hearing and feeling words on every page. If you are an aspiring author, this could be a good technique to emulate.

Summary

In this lesson we explored how to communicate influentially and build rapport with others, at both a conscious and an unconscious level.

The NLP 'core' model illustrates how everyone is unique, constructing their own personal 'map of the world' determined by internal 'filters'. Building rapport with someone creates a bridge to their world which enables a two-way spirit of co-operation to develop. The three elements of communication – body language (physiology), tone of voice and words – provide opportunities for matching and mirroring face to face, over the phone and in writing.

You now know whether you are predominantly a visual, hearing or feeling person and how to detect these different ways of thinking in others by observing their eye movements. By matching your vocabulary to the 'channel' in which the other person is thinking, you'll be able to 'speak their language' and thereby become more influential.

Fact-check (answers at the back)

1. How do we protect our conscious mind from overload?
   a) Through a set of 'filters' that are unique to each of us ❑
   b) By ignoring our memories ❑
   c) By using our unconscious mind with its unlimited capacity ❑
   d) By processing input from three senses only ❑

2. What do our filters do?
   a) Exclude painful thoughts ❑
   b) Separate us from others ❑
   c) Cause the conscious mind to become overloaded ❑
   d) Make sense of incoming information ❑

3. What's the fastest way to change our state of mind?
   a) Change our environment ❑
   b) Talk to someone with a different point of view ❑
   c) Change our physiology, or body language ❑
   d) We can't – our thoughts and emotions are fixed ❑

4. What is our 'map of the world'?
   a) Our unique way of seeing the world ❑
   b) What we make of others' memories ❑
   c) A three-dimensional map of our neighbourhood ❑
   d) How we visualize our thoughts ❑

5. Why is rapport important in communication?
   a) It's not important ❑
   b) People like to see others copying their movements ❑
   c) It makes us more aware of others' eye movements ❑
   d) It enables us to build a bridge to someone else's map of the world ❑

6. What are the three elements of communication?
   a) Physiology, tone of voice, words ❑
   b) Eye contact, handshake, written word ❑
   c) Dress code, smiling, gestures ❑
   d) Telephone, face to face, emails ❑

7. What makes up the smallest element of communication?
   a) Physiology ❑
   b) Words ❑
   c) Tone of voice ❑
   d) Pacing and leading ❑

8. When should you use pacing and leading?
   a) When you want to experiment with a new way of communicating ❑
   b) To mimic the other person's accent ❑
   c) To help calm down an angry person ❑
   d) When you can't match somebody's blink rate ❑

9. What is 'speaking somebody's language'?

a) Matching their key words ❑

b) Mimicking the other person's breathing rate ❑

c) Speaking more loudly if someone is quietly spoken ❑

d) Using the same tone of voice over the telephone ❑

10. What does VHF stand for?

a) Virtual, hearing, feeling ❑

b) Visual, hearsay, feedback loop ❑

c) Visual, hearing, feeling ❑

d) Viral, healing, falling ❑

LESSON 5

Filtered thinking

In the previous lesson we described how we take in the world around us and make sense of things by using our own personal set of 'filters'. Now we'll explore these filters in more depth and find out how to detect them in someone else. Using this information, we can influence that person in a way that is specifically appropriate to them.

The role of our filters is to sift through the huge volume of information we are constantly taking in through our five senses. Without these filters in place, our conscious mind, with its limited capacity, would be permanently in a state of overload. However, we often delete, distort or generalize from the information coming in to us.

Some of these filters act like software programs. Research has shown that we all have a set of 'either/or' programs that can be discovered conversationally. The main benefit of this is that, if you discover somebody's 'either/or' pattern, you can 'speak their language' by matching to it. Today you'll learn how to use your knowledge of filters to build further on the principles of rapport building, in order to influence more effectively.

'Software program' filters

Different people use different 'software program' filters when they filter or sort their experiences. We can divide these filters into several 'either/or' categories, as follows:

- Towards or away from
- Proactive or reactive
- Internal or external frame of reference
- Options or procedures
- Similarities or differences
- Global or detail
- Type A or type B.

Towards or away from?

This filter category relates to motivation and how people stay focused. Someone with a *towards* filter will know what they want and find it relatively easy to set goals and maintain a momentum towards achieving them. Someone with an *away from* filter may not know what they want, but they certainly know what they don't want. They know what they want to get away from and, like a magnet that repels, this can generate a good kick-start. However, the further they move away from the thing they want to get away from, the less powerful the motivation becomes. At that point, it is important to have a 'towards' goal in place, which is the magnet that attracts.

To detect which of these filters someone prefers, listen to their language. Do they talk about what they want to achieve, perhaps career progression or starting their own business? If so, this is a 'towards' person. To influence them, talk about how you might be able to help them achieve their goals.

Alternatively, do they talk about how much they hate their job, how they can't stand their colleagues and how much they want to get out? This indicates an 'away from' person. Empathize with them about their situation. How could you help them change it? It's also useful to explore with them what they would like instead, because they may well not have thought this through.

Which of these two filters do you most identify with – towards or away from?

Case study: George

George decided that he wanted to give up smoking. He had had enough of feeling wheezy and his clothes smelling of stale cigarette smoke, and the cost of buying cigarettes had become ridiculous. He was determined that he was not going to smoke any more. He started off well, managing a whole week without smoking, but, halfway through the second week, his resolve weakened and he found himself reaching for a cigarette.

What went wrong? George didn't have a 'towards' goal in place, so when the 'away from' motivation started to fade, there was nothing to take over from it and so it was easy to slip back into the behaviour he knew – smoking.

Proactive or reactive?

This filter category relates to taking action. The *proactive* person is someone who is typified by the Nike slogan, 'Just do it'. They often make snap decisions and then just jump in and get on with carrying out the appropriate action. A *reactive* person would rather hold back, consider all the alternatives and, ideally, wait for someone else to make the decision and initiate any actions to be taken.

Their different energy levels will often provide you with a clue to their preferred filter in this category. A proactive person will be energetic, possibly a multi-tasker with many projects on the go at once. A reactive person may have lower energy levels and be more likely to take the view that they can only do one thing at a time. They may even prefer someone else to prioritize their workload for them.

In terms of influencing and persuading these two, if what you are proposing sounds right, looks right and feels right to the proactive person, they will make a quick decision and want to go ahead as soon as possible.

For the reactive person, you would need to explore their decision-making strategy. What additional information do they need? Who else do they need to consult in order to make a decision? Beware of inadvertently applying pressure to the reactive person; just accept that, for them, making a decision needs to follow the more drawn-out, considered process that they feel comfortable with.

Which of these two filters do you most identify with – proactive or reactive?

Internal or external frame of reference?

This filter category correlates to personal self-esteem. An *internal* person has a good degree of self-confidence and can accurately assess how they are doing at any time. They know what is best for them and may resist a course of action that has been planned by somebody else if they feel it is not right for them. Because they have this degree of independent thinking, they are ideally suited to becoming entrepreneurs, running their own business without supervision.

An *external* person has a lower self-esteem. They depend on feedback from others as to how they are doing and need others to set standards for them. They are more comfortable being managed and supervised, and they need external reassurance in order to know that they are getting it right.

To detect the preferred filter, ask, 'How do you know when you've done something really well?' An internal person will tell you that they 'just know it' and they may not be able to be more specific than that. To influence, you could explore with them what would need to happen for them to experience that feeling of 'just knowing it' more often.

In answer to the same question, the external person will tell you all about some kind of 'hard' evidence. It might be achieving a quota or some other kind of measurement, or it might be that their manager has told them that they've done a good job. Explore with them what would need to happen for them to get that positive feedback more often.

Which of these two filters do you most identify with – internal or external?

Options or procedures?

This filter category strongly correlates to whether someone is right- or left-brain dominant – in other words, whether their natural inclination is to be creative (right-brain hemisphere) or logical (left-brain hemisphere).

An *options* person is right-brain dominant. They need to feel that they have choices and are free to develop alternatives, which could be quite innovative. They will be reluctant to follow a prescribed procedure, even if it has been successful in the past, because they will feel constrained and even bored. Their mind is constantly searching for a better way of doing things and so, if an organization needs to refresh or change the way it operates, an options person would be in their element tasked with such a project.

As a 'left-brainer', a *procedures* person's strength is in following to the letter a well-defined procedure or routine. Their attitude is, 'If it ain't broke, don't fix it,' and they will see no need to review or revise a way of doing something if it seems to be the 'right' way. In an environment where it is essential that established procedures are followed precisely – for example, if there is an element of safety involved – a procedures person will be a great asset.

To determine whether someone is an options or procedures person, ask them whether they prefer freedom or formality in the nature of their work. An options person will prefer freedom whereas a procedures person will feel more comfortable with formality.

An options person likes to challenge 'why' they are required to do something in a particular way and then to explore whether it could be done better another way. To influence them, engage them in this type of conversation, and then listen for their ideas!

A procedures person needs to know 'how' to do something and likes the answer to take the form of step-by-step, logical instructions. To influence, present your proposal in this format and it will make perfect sense to them.

Which of these two filters do you most identify with – options or procedures?

Similarities or differences?

Imagine that lying on a table in front of you are three highlighter pens. They are the same size and shape but with different-coloured inks – one is yellow, one is green and one is pink. Are they the same or different? Depending on your own filter, you may choose one of the following four answers:

- **Same** This means that you notice things that match, that are the same. People who have this filter like things to remain static. If they encounter change, it will push them out of their comfort zone and can make them feel unsettled. They are likely to remain in the same job and/or relationship for a long time. To influence them, focus on the importance of maintaining stability and how you can help them achieve this.
- **Same with differences** This means that you initially notice the similarities, then the differences. People with this filter are open to change but only if it evolves gradually, over time. A sudden change will disturb them. To influence them, talk about introducing change for the better over the longer term.

- **Different** This means that you could be a bit of a 'mismatcher'. People with this filter can be restless, constantly seeking variety. They may change jobs frequently and can easily become bored in a relationship. To influence them, offer them something new, innovative, cutting edge and different, but be aware that they will be looking for further updates in the future.
- **Different with similarities** This means that you first notice the differences, then the similarities. As with the 'different' people, change and variety will appeal to this type, but not to the same frequency. To influence them, explore what exactly triggers their desire for change and then match your proposal to that.

Which one of these four filters do you most identify with – same, same with differences, different, or different with similarities?

Global or detail?

This filter category relates to thinking patterns. The *global* person will be the 'big thinker', the visionary. They see the big picture – it's away in the distance and they have a strategy for getting there, which is along the lines of just heading off in that general direction and dealing with potential obstacles along the way as they arise.

The *detail* person is more comfortable dealing with small chunks of information. They like precision and are naturals for giving attention to detail, planning steps in sequence, with a comprehensive contingency plan in place in case of problems.

This filter is relatively easy to detect from a person's use of language. The global person will talk about their vision, their dream, often using the phrase 'big picture'. To have to get bogged down in detailed thinking and planning is anathema to them. To influence them, get completely caught up in their vision and then explore how you can help them achieve it without the tedium of dealing with all the nitty-gritty detail.

The detail person will tend to talk in a precise, measured way and may use the word 'steps', which defines the extent of their focus – just as far as the next step. They tend to be thorough and meticulous in their jobs and they gain a great sense of satisfaction from performing detailed work. To influence them, ask questions that drill down into the level of detail that they love and then explore any challenges they have in carrying out their work in this exacting style.

Which of these two filters do you most identify with – global or detail?

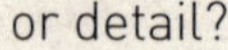

By identifying your own and other people's preferred filters, you will be able to understand others better. Then you can adapt your behaviour so that you work with them from a position of rapport rather than conflict.

Type A or type B?

Similar to global and detail filters, these two working styles can become a source of friction in the workplace if a strong type A and a strong type B are working together. However, for a team to work effectively, it is important to have a mixture of the two.

Complete the following questionnaire to discover your preferred working style. Read each pair of statements and tick the one (either A or B) with which you identify most closely. Then count up your scores for A and B statements. Which of these two working styles do you most identify with – type A or type B?

A statement		B statement	
I'm competitive – winning is very important to me.	❑	I just enjoy playing the game. If I win, it's a bonus.	❑
I sometimes get impatient when others are talking and I may interrupt.	❑	I always allow others time to finish what they're saying.	❑
At my best I'm assertive although, under pressure, I may become aggressive.	❑	I'm easy-going, and I tend to be more passive than aggressive.	❑
I tend to speak quickly and quite loudly.	❑	I think before I speak and then talk in a measured, deliberate way.	❑
I hate wasting time; I'm a fast mover and like to multi-task.	❑	I like to take things at a steady pace. I'm a slow, deliberate mover.	❑
Planning is boring. I like to think big, be spontaneous and just go for it.	❑	It's important to work to a plan, with the 'T's crossed and the 'I's dotted.	❑
I find it hard to relax completely – I like to keep myself occupied.	❑	I find it easy just to do nothing but relax.	❑
I'm ambitious, an achiever and eager for promotion.	❑	I enjoy where I am now in my career and prefer to take life as it comes.	❑
I leave things until the last minute and do my best work under pressure.	❑	I always ensure that I start things with plenty of time to meet deadlines.	❑
I rarely allow contingency time for travel and can end up rushed and late.	❑	I leave plenty of time for travel, I'm very punctual and I'm never late.	❑
I tend to hide my emotions and feelings; they can be a sign of weakness.	❑	I'm happy to express my emotions and feelings – we're all human.	❑
I deliver a good standard of work and I'm respected for it.	❑	I am a perfectionist. It consumes my time and is not always appreciated.	❑
I can be impatient; I want results now.	❑	Everything comes to those who wait.	❑

Type A

If you scored more As than Bs, this indicates that you have a type-A working style. You may be quite driven, prone to working harder, faster and longer hours than your colleagues.

You strive to be an achiever on as many different fronts as possible and this can result in you taking on far more work than you can realistically handle. You hate wasting time; if you have a doctor's appointment, you will take a book to read in the waiting room. If you are watching television, you may also be reading a newspaper or doing the ironing at the same time. The thought of going on a relaxing beach holiday without access to a mobile phone or the Internet is anathema to you. Needless to say, type As are prone to stress and this stress can be self-induced – by their lifestyle.

If you are a type A, you need to take a step back and look at the balance that exists between work, family and you (hobbies, relaxation and health). If there is a significant imbalance, particularly if work is dominating your life, you need to take steps to redress that situation. Remember that an accumulation of stress can lead to serious health problems. There is no need to feel guilty and no need to keep on proving how good or effective you are.

- Set realistic goals for yourself, both at work and at home, and then plan exactly how you will achieve them.
- Delegate those things that you cannot realistically achieve and be prepared to turn down new projects rather than overcommitting yourself.
- Use 'to do' lists to focus your energies at work and avoid that 'headless chicken' feeling.
- Learn to relax more.
- Make sure that you leave work at a reasonable time, share more time with your family and friends, and aim to become physically fitter.

Type B

If you scored more Bs than As, you have a type-B working style. You like to achieve things in your own way and at your own pace, rather like the tortoise in the fable of the hare and the tortoise. You are happy working in a team but may find it difficult to say no to colleagues. You will tend to avoid confrontation and conflict although, if pushed, you can be assertive. You take great pride in your work but can go overboard on quality at times. You can become so engrossed in researching some small detail that you end up as the world's expert on it. This consumes time and may be inappropriate if a deadline is looming. Type Bs often lack clear goals in work, career and life in general; however, this can help to keep their stress levels under control.

If you are a type B, you need to set quantifiable goals for yourself that can be objectively measured.

- Beware of trying to do everything to perfection – it is too time-consuming. Assess an appropriate standard of quality, deliver to that level and stop there.
- Be prepared to express your opinions when necessary, even if they may be in conflict with those of someone else. If you are assertive and maintain respect for others, you will be respected also.
- Become more decisive and stop procrastinating.
- Try to see the 'big picture'. It is very easy for a type B to get so bogged down in compiling intricate plans that nothing is accomplished.

Summary

Today we explored how 'filters' act like software programs – defining how we think, feel and behave. As stated yesterday, everybody's set of filters is unique to them and there is no right or wrong preference – our preferences may just be different from those held by others. You have learned how to recognize every set of 'either/or' filters (in yourself and others) and how to match to them in terms of speaking the 'right' language in order to influence.

To become a 'filter detective', engage people in conversation using some of the language cues (questions) listed for each pair of filters and seek to determine their preferences. If you are doing this with friends or colleagues, share your findings with them to see whether they agree with you.

Through the questionnaire, you will have discovered whether you have a type-A or type-B working style. These styles are similar to the global/detail filters, so you may have noticed a correlation between your global/detail result and whether you are predominantly a type A or type B.

Fact-check (answers at the back)

1. How does awareness of filters help us influence?
   a) By enabling us to empathize with and understand other people ❑
   b) By identifying the information we are constantly taking in ❑
   c) By taking advantage of other people's ways of thinking ❑
   d) By helping us share the detailed plans of the other person ❑

2. What does the towards/away from filter relate to?
   a) Motivation ❑
   b) Body language ❑
   c) Setting goals ❑
   d) Being competitive ❑

3. What characterizes reactive people?
   a) A tendency to be quite lazy ❑
   b) An ability to multi-task ❑
   c) Spontaneity ❑
   d) A preference for others to make their decisions for them ❑

4. What characterizes people with an internal frame of reference?
   a) A need for plenty of praise from their manager ❑
   b) Good self-esteem ❑
   c) A need for hard evidence of their achievements ❑
   d) A preference for working indoors ❑

5. What characterizes an options person?
   a) Their constant search for a better way of doing things ❑
   b) Their need for step-by-step, logical instructions ❑
   c) A liking for following established procedures ❑
   d) A preference for working in a structured way ❑

6. What does a similarities filter indicate?
   a) A constant search for variety ❑
   b) The person will notice things that match ❑
   c) A desire for innovation ❑
   d) The person will like to change jobs frequently ❑

7. What does a global person like to do?
   a) Frequent international travel ❑
   b) Have big ideas ❑
   c) Plan every step towards the achievement of their goals ❑
   d) Speak in a precise, measured way ❑

8. What is a tendency of type-A people?
   a) To take life as it comes ❑
   b) To correlate to the detail filter ❑
   c) To be the 'big picture' thinkers ❑
   d) To love perfectionism ❑

9. What is a tendency of type-B people?

a) To be very competitive ❑
b) To find it easy to relax and just do nothing ❑
c) To be short of time and often late ❑
d) To be perfectionists ❑

10. Why is it useful to be able to detect someone's filters?

a) So you can 'speak their language' and influence them ❑
b) So you can put the same types into the same team ❑
c) In order to avoid the people who are different from you ❑
d) In order to tell them how to change ❑

LESSON 6

Flexible influencing

You can use several further NLP techniques to enable you to develop more flexibility in your influencing and persuasion methods.

In this lesson we shall look at some of the 'presuppositions' or 'excellence beliefs' upon which NLP has been built and see how operating within these beliefs can improve your success. We'll also explore some of the NLP language techniques that work particularly well when influencing. We will review the importance of having empowering beliefs in place when you are aiming to increase your ability to influence well, and how your own language may be undermining your belief in yourself.

Finally, you will learn how to create a 'future history' through a specific visualization technique. This technique allows you to visualize a future event unfolding in exactly the way you want it to, in order to help you generate a good outcome in reality. You can use the technique in advance of any situation in which you need to be at your influential best.

The power of 'excellence beliefs'

NLP was first developed in the 1970s as a study of excellence, with top achievers such as Walt Disney being researched and 'modelled' so that their tried-and-tested techniques for success could be learned and used by others. It is now accepted globally as one of the most powerful and effective personal development methodologies available. Working within its 'principles of excellence' or presuppositions, listed below, can strengthen your communications and in turn improve your power to persuade and influence others.

'The person with the most flexible behaviour can have the most influence on an outcome.'

This 'excellence belief' means that, if your strategy is to have a number of different approaches planned in advance, then you can easily switch between them to achieve a desired outcome. By contrast, if you have planned only one route to your goal and an obstacle occurs that blocks this route, you will not achieve your goal. This attitude is typical in people who say things like, 'It's my way or the highway.' In other words, if others do not 'buy into' their views, they have no fallback option as an alternative.

'The meaning of communication is the response it elicits.'

In any communication, whether one to one or one to many, the only way you can know how you are doing is by noticing the feedback you are getting. You will probably have experienced this, perhaps if you were explaining something a little complicated to another person and you noticed a puzzled expression on their face. You instinctively realized that they did not understand what you just said, so you might have continued with, 'In other words...' and then explained it again in a different way. When their response changed to one of comprehension, indicated perhaps with a slight smile and nod of the head, this told you that your message was understood.

During any kind of influencing scenario, it is essential that you are continually noticing the feedback you are getting from your audience.

The fastest way to change your state of mind is to change your body language. If you are feeling nervous before a presentation or meeting, choose to adopt upright, open, confident-looking body language and it will *have a positive effect on how you feel. You could say that this is 'fake it 'til you make it', but if it works, why not?*

'If you always do what you've always done, you will always get what you've always got. So if what you're doing isn't working, do something different.'

Einstein's definition of insanity was 'doing the same thing over and over and expecting to get different results'. If, for example, your presentation that you hoped would influence and persuade didn't work the first time, there is a strong chance that it will fall short next time also. Revisit it, review it, revise it – do whatever it takes, but make sure you do something differently in order to generate a different result.

'There is no such thing as failure; there is only feedback.'

Imagine that you have an important meeting with a senior director in your organization. Your objective is to present your ideas for a radical new product or service that you are passionate about and which you would like your organization to adopt. You think it goes well but the director rejects your proposal. You leave the meeting feeling that you have failed.

You didn't fail. In fact, all that happened was that you got a result that wasn't the one you wanted. Instead, what you actually got was a valuable learning opportunity. Use it well and then do something different next time. When things go the way we expect them to, we learn nothing. When things *don't* go the way we want them to, they present fabulous opportunities to learn and grow. Allow your mind to formulate an answer to this question: 'What would you do if you *knew* you couldn't fail?'

'If one person can do it, others can too.'

This presupposition reflects the fundamental principle of NLP, that of modelling excellence in others. Think of someone you know who has influencing abilities that you admire. What exactly are they doing to be so persuasive, and how could you adopt their techniques for yourself? And then think of others whom you admire, and do the same thing. Model their excellence and you will be able to replicate their success.

Modelling excellence: the four-minute mile

Before 1954, when Roger Bannister became the first person to run a mile in under four minutes, many 'experts', including doctors, had confidently stated that it was impossible for a human being to achieve this feat. They said that their heart would explode, their lungs would collapse and their shinbones would shatter. Perhaps not surprisingly, the previous record of four minutes 1.4 seconds had stood for nine years, because who would want to have all these awful things happen to them? However, Bannister, himself a junior doctor as well as an athlete, decided not only that it was possible but that he was the man to do it.

The record he set, of three minutes 59.4 seconds, stood for just 46 days until it was broken and it has since been broken by many more athletes. In the last 50 years the record has been lowered by almost 17 seconds, and it is now estimated that well in excess of 1,000 athletes have run a mile in under four minutes.

'Resistance in someone you wish to influence is a sign of lack of rapport.'

The better the rapport you have with someone, the more productive the conversation will be and the easier it will be to influence them. If you sense from the feedback you are receiving from the other person that there is some kind of unseen barrier between you, there is a strong chance that rapport is missing. Lesson 4 focused on rapport building using the principles of matching and mirroring body language, tone of voice and words. It might be that, in your keenness to start influencing, you skipped over this important step. Remember that you need to build a bridge across to the other person's 'map of the world'. Without this bridge in place, there is little or no connection.

'The mind and body are part of the same structure and affect each other.'

The power of body language

Here's a short exercise for you: sit up straight in your chair, look up at the ceiling, hold a big smile on your face and, staying like that, try to feel really miserable.

How was that? Did you manage to feel really miserable? Perhaps not, so let's try the opposite to see if that is any easier. This time, slump down in your chair, look down at the floor, hold a really 'long' expression on your face and try to feel really happy.

Was that a success? You probably could not do it. So what is going on? The mind and body are inextricably linked and will always reflect each other's 'states'. In this exercise, you first adopted a body language that reflected happy thoughts and feelings, and then tried to create a state of mind – miserable – in complete opposition to that body language. In that conflict, probably the body language won. Similarly, the body language probably won again when you adopted a 'miserable' body language and tried to feel happy.

The exercise above deliberately asked you to *try* to feel an emotion that was in conflict with your body language. Your mind interpreted this as 'try and fail'. The word 'try' has a get-out clause in it. If this is a word you use in your vocabulary, you are setting yourself up to fail. It is much better to say what you *will* do rather than what you will *try* to do.

In a similar fashion, your mind cannot process a negative command because it doesn't understand what it is not supposed to do. For example, whatever you do now, don't think about a yellow door. Now, what are you thinking about? Perhaps a yellow door? If you use the word 'don't' in your vocabulary, you may well get the opposite result to the one you want. To achieve a better outcome, always say what you *do* want rather than what you *don't* want.

People will stereotype you within four seconds according to your visual appearance so, if your body language is in any way negative or uncertain, this will set the scene for you before you have spoken a single word.

'There is a solution to every problem.'

This inspiring excellence belief tells us that, no matter what the problem is, there is always a solution – we just may not have discovered it yet. While it may not be the 'ideal' solution, nevertheless, it is a solution. For example, in the course of running my business, I have occasionally had clients who didn't pay my invoices and then went bust. The solution I would have liked was to be paid the money they owed me but, because these companies had stopped trading, that just wasn't going to happen. The actual solution was to write off the debts, put those clients behind me and move on with my business. All the time that we hold on to a problem, we are holding on to a potential stressor. We must therefore seek alternatives that will resolve the problem and give us closure with it.

Memory and imagination

'Memory and imagination use the same neurological circuits and can potentially have the same impact on the individual.'

Because memory and imagination use the same neurological circuits, your mind cannot tell the difference between a remembered activity and an imagined one, which means that if you visualize something vividly enough, your mind thinks it is looking at a memory. And your mind believes that if you've already carried out this activity in the past, then you can do it again.

Visualization: Linford Christie

In 1992, British sprinter Linford Christie won the 100m gold medal at the Barcelona Olympic Games, becoming at 32 years of age the oldest athlete to have achieved this feat. As part of his training, he had worked with a visualization of running down an imaginary tunnel on the stimulus of the sound of the starting gun. The purpose of the tunnel in the visualization was to eliminate all other visual distractions such as the other competitors and the crowd. The auditory stimulus was the 'B' of the 'bang' from the gun.

In his mind, Christie had run this race hundreds of times and, of course, he had won it every time, so when he lined up on the starting blocks that day, there was no doubt in his mind that he was about to replicate his imagined, gold-medal-winning performance. And so he did.

This is the reason why so many outstanding performers, whether in sport, business or other arenas, attribute their success to visualization. Roger Bannister visualized himself running the four-minute mile. Boxer Muhammad Ali would create what he called 'future history' by visualizing every round of a forthcoming boxing match in minute detail and then predicting the round in which he would knock out his opponent. He would then take great delight in announcing this to his opponent prior to the fight commencing, along with his affirmation, 'I am the greatest.'

How to create a winning visualization

If you have a meeting or presentation coming up at which you need to be at your influential best, then create a visualization of the event unfolding exactly the way you want it to and keep running through it as a mental rehearsal. For the best results, incorporate the following points:

1. You need to be fully 'associated' with it, so imagine that you are seeing the event through your own eyes, as if it is going on around you.
2. Break the event down into stages and build a checkpoint into each one. For example, when you enter the room where the event is to take place, who is the first person to greet you and what exactly will they say? What would be the next stage and what checkpoint could you create for that? And so on.
3. The more sensory information you can incorporate, the better. What do you see? What does the room look like? What are you wearing? What do you hear? Include specific words that the other people there would say, such as 'impressive' or 'this sounds really good'. How are you feeling? Confident? Relaxed? Include whatever feelings are appropriate. Even include smell and taste if you can – perhaps you would be drinking a cup of coffee or a glass of water. If so, include these.
4. Imagine that the final part is the successful outcome that you want to achieve. Build in exactly how that will feel and imagine how you will congratulate yourself on a job well done.

Influencing through language

When we speak, we are usually conveying a shortened, simplified and generalized version of what we are thinking. In so doing, we often leave out or even distort some of the information, which leads to misunderstandings and to some important facts being withheld.

Much of the language adopted in NLP was modelled from well-known psychiatrist and hypnotherapist Milton Erickson, who was able to facilitate phenomenal changes in his clients conversationally. The NLP 'meta model' uses language to clarify meaning and thus ensure that you gain a clear understanding of the words used by others. The benefit of using the meta model is that it helps you to gain a better understanding of what somebody is *really* saying. Because a person will always be speaking through the filters of their own personal map of the world, we may often be unsure about what they really mean. However, we can clarify what they mean by asking specific questions. This will then enable us to be far more effective as an influencer.

The following are elements of the NLP meta model.

Unspecified nouns

This is where we replace the noun in a sentence with words such as 'they' or 'it', or where the noun is implied rather than specified. To gain a more accurate understanding, ask questions such as 'Who or what, specifically?' For example:

- 'They are making a decision today.' 'Who are?'
- 'It's always been done this way.' 'What, specifically?'

Unspecified verbs

This follows the same principle as unspecified nouns, but here it is the verbs used that fail to convey enough information to get across the full message. In this case, ask, 'How, specifically?' For example:

- 'I was helped to do this.' 'How, specifically?'
- 'Just get on and do it.' 'How, specifically?'

Comparisons

Comparisons are often used in advertisements, for example when a product is described as 'better' without the ad saying what it is being compared with. Clarify by asking, 'Compared with what?' For example:

- 'This one is better.' 'Better than what?'
- 'He was at his worst today.' 'Compared with what?'

Judgements

These are similar to comparisons, in that a view is expressed without specifying whose view it is. Clarify by asking questions to establish whose judgement it is and/or on what basis the judgement has been made. For example:

- 'This is the best one on the market.' 'By what criteria is it the best?'
- 'This does the best job.' 'In whose opinion?'

Nominalizations

Also called abstract nouns, nominalizations are nouns that started off as verbs. As nouns they are vaguer and more intangible than the original active verb. A verb such as 'educate' becomes a static noun ('education'). To clarify its meaning, turn the nominalization back into a verb and ask for qualifying information. For example:

- 'I received a good education at home.' 'Who educated you? How did they do that?'
- 'We had lengthy discussions.' 'What did you discuss?'

Modal operators of possibility

These are words that reflect our beliefs around what is and is not possible for us. They may well reflect limiting beliefs and can be explored by asking, 'What would happen if you did?' or 'What stops you?' For example:

- 'I can't present in public.' 'What would happen if you did?'
- 'I can't speak to him.' 'What stops you?'

Modal operators of necessity

These are similar to the possibility words but they reflect needs rather than beliefs. They can be explored using similar questions as for modal operators of possibility. For example:

- 'I must be the last to leave the office.' 'What would happen if you weren't?'
- 'I ought to learn how to do that.' 'What would happen if you didn't?'

Universal quantifiers

These are sweeping generalizations that allow for no exceptions. They utilize words such as 'all', 'every', 'always' and 'never' and can be challenged by reflecting them back or by asking about any possible exceptions. For example:

- 'I never remember people's names.' 'Never? Has there ever been a time when you did remember a name?'
- 'I always make bad decisions.' 'Always? Have you ever made a decision that wasn't bad?'

Complex equivalence

This is when two statements are linked to imply that they mean the same thing, but they may well be based on an incorrect assumption. Clarify the statements by asking how one statement 'means' the other one. For example:

- 'He doesn't attend our weekly meetings any more ... he must be too busy.' 'How does his lack of attendance necessarily mean that he is too busy?'
- 'She never rings me any more ... I must have offended her.' 'How does her not ringing you mean you've offended her?'

Presuppositions

Presuppositions – a term also used to mean beliefs that underpin NLP – imply, in the context of language, assumptions that may or may not be correct. Clarify such an assumption by asking, 'What leads you to believe that...?' For example:

- 'Would you like the blue one or the red one?' 'What leads you to believe that I wish to purchase either of them?'
- 'When you go to the meeting, what will you say?' 'What makes you think I'm going? How do you know I'm going to speak?'

Cause and effect

Although similar to complex equivalence, in cause and effect one statement is taken to have caused the other one. This can reflect an inappropriate 'blame' being allocated, especially if emotions are involved. For example, 'You make me so angry when you do that' implies that one person has complete control over another person's emotions, whereas the reality is that we all choose our own emotions. Clarify the statement by asking exactly how one element has caused the other one. For example:

- 'I'd like to exercise more but I don't have the time.' 'What would have to happen for you to have the time to exercise?'
- 'I was going to say something but I knew he'd take it the wrong way.' 'How do you know he'd take what you said the wrong way?'

Mind reading

This is where one person presumes that they know what another person is thinking. We often base our presumptions on how we ourselves would be thinking or feeling in the same situation and we project it on to the other person. Alternatively, it could be the result of a misinterpretation of the other person's body language. We can ask for clarification by saying, 'How exactly do you know...?' For example:

- 'I know you don't like my idea.' 'How exactly do you know that?'
- 'She's ignoring me.' 'How can you be sure?'

Summary

In this lesson we have drawn on some of the key principles of NLP in order to incorporate flexibility into your influencing style. The more flexible you can be, the better equipped you will be to 'think on your feet' during any interaction in which you need to influence others.

The quality of your language will determine the quality of your results. You discovered how the elimination of words such as 'try' and 'don't' can make profound positive differences to your outcomes, and you saw how you can filter language not only to influence others but also to influence yourself.

You also discovered how to create and use an effective visualization, a technique used by highly successful people as a mental rehearsal for their achievements.

We also explored the meta model of language, which employs questioning to clarify what others are saying, avoid misunderstandings and open up opportunities for influential conversation.

Fact-check (answers at the back)

1. What does NLP stand for?
a) Neuro-linguistic procedures ❑
b) New language perception ❑
c) Neuro-linguistic programming ❑
d) Neurotic language principles ❑

2. What's the best way to ensure that your message is understood?
a) By ignoring the feedback – it's unnecessary when you are communicating with someone ❑
b) By repeating it more loudly until it is understood ❑
c) By noticing the feedback you are getting and adjusting your message accordingly ❑
d) Trying again later by going over it again in the same way ❑

3. What is the best way to achieve a goal?
a) By having several possible routes to that goal ❑
b) With one good, well-thought-out route ❑
c) By keeping on with what you are doing, even if it doesn't work first time ❑
d) By being content with any result, even if it isn't the one you wanted ❑

4. What's the best way to think about a problem?
a) Some problems have no solution ❑
b) There is a solution to every problem, although it may not be the ideal one ❑
c) Holding on to a problem is a stress-free option ❑
d) Solutions must be ideal, or they are no solution at all ❑

5. How did athletes break Roger Bannister's four-minute mile record?
a) By modelling excellence ❑
b) By ignoring the naysayers ❑
c) By competing with one another ❑
d) By improving their fitness ❑

6. How can you tell whether you have achieved rapport with someone?
a) They show resistance to your ideas ❑
b) They start to match and mirror your body language ❑
c) You have made physical contact with them ❑
d) You feel that you can read their mind ❑

7. What's the fastest way to change your state of mind?
a) Ask your mind to process a negative command ❑
b) Change your body language ❑
c) Leave the room and do something else for a few minutes ❑
d) Say what you don't want in order to get what you do want ❑

8. Why should you never have the word 'try' in your influencing vocabulary?
a) It makes you look weak ❑
b) The mind can't process it ❑
c) It's too vague ❑
d) The mind interprets 'try' as 'try and fail' ❑

9. What's the NLP meta model?
a) A way of disguising your feelings ❑
b) A method of getting along with people ❑
c) A way of using language to clarify language ❑
d) A modelling technique ❑

10. What is visualization?
a) A mental rehearsal of a future situation ❑
b) Seeing yourself running down a tunnel ❑
c) Sensory overload ❑
d) Daydreaming ❑

LESSON 7

Proven persuasion techniques

In this lesson we will explore a range of proven persuasion techniques that will further enhance everything you have learned so far.

Listening is an essential communication skill and a key skill in influencing. A good listener will easily detect all the cues (which could be buying signals) in the other person and then just match their proposal to their needs. You will discover the three levels of listening and which one never to use if you want to influence someone.

You'll also learn about two tried and tested persuasion formulae – FAB and AIDA – and how to incorporate them into marketing and sales activities, including conversations.

Significant research has been conducted on which words are the most influential and are therefore used most often in 'persuasive literature'. Now you'll learn why each of these top 15 words works so well. Some of them will be obvious but others may surprise you.

In Lesson 4 we looked at 'convincers' and the power of three. We will explore some additional convincers and other 'emotional triggers' here that have been proven to work well in situations such as networking events.

The three levels of listening

While hearing is a function (you have ears and they detect sounds), listening is a skill. The more you develop this skill, the better a communicator and an influencer you will become. There are three different levels of listening, as follows:

- **Level 1 – internal listening**
  At this level, the listener is focused on him/herself. They are interpreting whatever is being said in terms of what it means to them. If it brings something to mind, they will interrupt the speaker in order to share that thought. This is a very selfish type of listening; continually interrupting someone else is extremely disrespectful. *Never* use level 1 if you want to influence someone.
- **Level 2 – focused listening**
  This is attentive listening, with the focus on the speaker. The listener may be leaning forward, engrossed in the conversation. They will notice the speaker's body language, tone of voice and words, as well as elements such as energy, expression, what is being not just said but also implied, and so on. This is a good type of listening to use if you are in a one-to-one situation.
- **Level 3 – global listening**
  Also known as 360° listening, the speaker is being listened to as if part of a wider environment. The listener is using their intuition to sense 'signals' and to take in all information available. (The best stand-up comedians use this type of listening to interact with their audience and to know the exact moment to drop in their punchline for the greatest effect.) This is the best level to use if you are making a presentation to a group of people that you want to influence.

As with any skill, the more you practise effective listening, the more competent – and influential – you will become.

FAB statements

Everyone's favourite radio station is WIIFM, or 'What's in it for me?' This means that, whatever it is that you want to convey in your influencing conversation, the other party must be able to see some benefit, and be able to sense that benefit quite quickly in order to stay interested. One technique that achieves this very effectively is the FAB statement.

FAB stands for Feature, Advantage and Benefit. The statement is structured as follows:

- **Feature** – here you say what a product or service is or focus on a specific aspect of it: 'Because...'
- **Advantage** – this describes what that product/service/aspect does: 'It can/you can...'
- **Benefit** – this explains why the advantage is a really good thing to have: 'which means that...'

An example is: '*Because* this mobile phone has a camera function, *it can* take photographs and even short video clips, *which means that* you will never miss a photo opportunity again.'

FAB statements incorporate the conventional 'features and benefits' format but, with the addition of the 'advantage' element, two levels of benefits are being presented, which makes it even more persuasive. It is always a good idea to have several FAB statements prepared in advance of any situation in which you may need to influence others. Use a table like the one below to create three examples for yourself. For each one, think of a particular aspect of your product or service, ideally one that is unique to you or your organization.

Feature	Advantage	Benefit
1 Because...	it can/you can...	which means that...
2 Because...	it can/you can...	which means that...
3 Because...	it can/you can...	which means that...

Having a variety of FAB statements prepared will give you flexibility. Depending on the cues you pick up from the other person by listening attentively to them, you will be able to choose the appropriate statement to use. It may be that they have outlined a problem they have; if you can phrase your FAB statement so that it sounds exactly like the solution they need, they are likely to be very interested in what you have to offer.

AIDA

Another formula with a proven track record in terms of influencing people to respond to marketing communications is AIDA. (This has nothing to do with Verdi's opera of the same name, although that connection does help to make the acronym more memorable.) The letters stand for Attention, Interest, Desire and Action:

- **Attention**
  Attract the attention of the reader by making a bold statement that is relevant to them and that will generate awareness of your product or service, or of a problem that they may not have realized they have.
- **Interest**
  Raise interest by focusing on and demonstrating advantages and benefits (rather than promoting features, as in traditional advertising).
- **Desire**
  Convince the reader that they really want your product/service and that it will satisfy their needs or solve their problem.
- **Action**
  Tell the reader what to do next; what action must they take now in order to buy your product or take you up on your offer?

For example:

- **Attention**
  Do you have any old mobile phones lying around that you no longer use?
- **Interest**
  Did you know that they could be worth a significant amount of money?
- **Desire**
  We buy old mobiles and will pay you a good price for yours.

- **Action**
  Go to our website now and check out how much yours is worth. Then simply post it to us and you will receive a cheque by return.

This formula also works well in letter format, in which case each letter of AIDA would comprise one paragraph, building up to the call to action.

The 15 most influential words in marketing

Research has shown that certain words are extremely effective for influencing people, especially if they communicate at both the conscious and unconscious levels of the mind simultaneously. The following list of words, compiled by Kerry L. Johnson and reproduced here with his kind permission, have been shown to be the most influential. If you look at advertising in magazines and newspapers and on advertising hoardings and billboards, and listen to television and radio adverts, you will see and hear these words being used repeatedly.

Word	Effect
1 Discover	This generates interest, evokes a feeling of opportunity and suggests a better life.
2 Good	This is not a high-powered word, which is the secret of its success; it evokes stability and security. If something is good for your clients, they will want to buy it. If it's good, it's not bad. Everyone wants to be associated with what's good.
3 Money	Few people feel they have enough and everyone wants more.
4 Easy	What everyone wants is more simplicity and the ability to do things more easily. If your product can make something easier for potential purchasers, they will be more likely to buy it.
5 Guaranteed	Most people fear taking a risk. They want to know that, if your product doesn't work out, they can get their money back.
6 Health	'If I've got my health, I've got everything.' If a product promises financial, emotional or physical health, it offers a big plus. To many people, this is more important than money.

(Continued)

Word	Effect
7 Love	Said to 'make the world go round', love is important in everyone's life and is a prime selling enticement.
8 New	If it's new, it must be better, improved and at the 'cutting edge'. Unless a product is specifically targeted to evoke nostalgia, anyone trying to sell something old-fashioned meets with limited success.
9 Proven	Although we like new things, we want reliability as well. We want something that has been tested and proven not to be harmful in any way. We need to know that it will neither break down nor require a lot of servicing. We don't want to doubt that something will work.
10 Results	We want to know exactly what we're getting for spending our money.
11 Safe	This closely parallels health. We all value our lives and if a product is safe, or our assets are safe, we are much more trusting.
12 Save	Saving money is almost as important as making money. If a company can't promise that you will make money with a product, it usually promises to help you save money. Saving is better than spending.
13 Own	We all like to own things. Owning is better than buying because it implies possession rather than more spending. When you present a product, talk about owning it rather than buying it.
14 Free	We love to say that you can't get something for nothing, but we don't believe it! 'Free' is an instant eye-catcher, something that compels you to look or listen further. If you can use the word 'free', pointing out that your customer will get something for nothing, you will get that customer's attention immediately.
15 Best	If you know that a product has been shown to be the best in any way, shape or form, be sure to make your customer aware of it. Something that has been shown to be the best in any context exerts a powerful pull on us to possess it for ourselves.

Because all these words work so well, both in writing and verbally, keep a list of them by your telephone so that you can drop them into a conversation and thus become instantly more influential!

Using persuasion techniques

Select some of the advantages and benefits that you identified in the FAB statement exercise and draft a letter or email that incorporates the AIDA formula, using just a short paragraph for each element. Use as many of the 15 words as possible, without making the end result too lengthy.

More convincers

In Lesson 4 you discovered that people have preferred channels of communication – visual, hearing or feeling. Not only will they speak in these channels, but they also like to be communicated with, and influenced, in their preferred channel. If you are in a one-to-one situation and you become aware from listening to the other person's language and watching their eye movements which channel they fit into, then you will need to think about the following:

- **Visual people**
  What evidence do they need to see in order to be convinced? Can you show them examples, pictures, charts, diagrams, or even a short video clip? Don't use long verbal explanations with visual people, because they will lose interest quickly. They will also notice your appearance in far more detail than hearing or feeling people, so be meticulous about how you present yourself.
- **Hearing people**
  What do they need to hear from you to be convinced? Hearing people like to be 'talked through' things in steps, procedures and sequences, so structure your presentation in that way. Also, vary your voice tonality, speed and volume, as this will appeal more to them.
- **Feeling people**
  What do they need to feel in order to be convinced? These people will go with their gut feeling and they like to be tactile when evaluating something. If you can give them a sample of your product to touch, they will appreciate that. They are

'hands-on' learners, so if you can demonstrate something to them and then give them the chance to have a go for themselves, this will work well. Feeling people will notice the quality of a handshake, so make sure that yours is firm without being a bone-crusher.

The law of reciprocity

It is human nature that when someone has done us a good turn, we feel a need to reciprocate and do something for them. This is known as the law of reciprocity. In terms of communication, if you show a genuine interest in somebody by asking them questions and listening attentively to their replies, there will more than likely come a point at which they will say something like, 'So what about you? What do you do?' People like to be listened to (this is the 'good turn' you are doing for them), so on no account lapse into level 1 listening.

In his book *7 Habits of Highly Effective People* (1989), Stephen Covey defines habit number 5 as 'Seek first to understand, then to be understood'. He states that most people listen with the intent to reply rather than to understand, and this affects the quality of their listening. He also says that we tend to be keen to put our point across and be understood rather than first wanting to understand the other person. If you find yourself at a networking event, you will see this happening constantly. If you make sure that you are the person who asks questions and really listens to the answers, you will make a very positive impression on the other attendees.

The law of scarcity

If we think something is in short supply, we want it. Even if it is only rumoured that there could be a shortage of a particular commodity, we may feel a need to 'stock up' in case it runs out altogether. You will have seen this happening with, for example, petrol. If it is reported in the media that service stations may run short of fuel for some reason, immediately queues will form. People will sit in their cars in a queue for an hour or two (burning fuel), sometimes just to top up an almost-full tank.

As a result, the service station runs out of fuel and the rumoured shortage becomes a reality.

How could you use this 'law'? If you are launching a promotion of some kind, think about imposing some limitations to create scarcity and thereby increase desire. For example:

- 'Only seven places remaining!'
- 'Offer must close at midnight on Friday!'
- 'Discontinued model – only two left at this price!'

Emotional triggers

Just as we tend to buy what we *want* rather than just what we *need*, so emotions play a key part in influencing our behaviour. For instance, Bob Geldof activated our emotions and feelings of guilt with his Live Aid appeal, raising £40 million to help alleviate suffering and starvation in Ethiopia.

Another curious and amusing example of an emotional trigger is the interesting phenomenon of cute cat pictures becoming widespread on the Internet. Several different, corroborative sources now suggest that, if you have a business page on Facebook and you would like to attract more visitors, posting a photo of a cat on there will do the trick! Yes, honestly. I suspect a photo of a cute kitten sitting on your keyboard may be even better, but apparently this works. Do with this as you will!

Summary

In this lesson you have learned some proven practical and effective persuasion techniques.

To be influential, we have to know how to communicate successfully. One of the most important communication skills is the ability to listen well. If you identified yourself as a level 1 listener, you now know that this is a skill you need to practise!

The FAB and AIDA techniques also work well, so familiarize yourself with them so that they will come naturally to you in an influencing conversation. It's also worth learning how and when to use the 15 most influential words.

By presenting information to people via their preferred channel of communication, you can increase your powers of persuasion. The laws of reciprocity and scarcity and emotional triggers also present opportunities to be influential.

Fact-check (answers at the back)

1. What is level 3 listening?
   a) Speaking more than listening ❑
   b) The best one to use in a one-to-one conversation ❑
   c) The best one to use when presenting to a group of people ❑
   d) Being focused on your own internal dialogue ❑

2. What does FAB stand for?
   a) Feature, Advantage, Benefit ❑
   b) Feature, Adaptability, Brightness ❑
   c) Fitness, Advancement, Benevolence ❑
   d) Flexibility, Assistance, Benison ❑

3. What does AIDA stand for?
   a) Administration, Influence, Design, Action ❑
   b) Audience, Interest, Designer, Animation ❑
   c) Attendance, Individuality, Desire, Activity ❑
   d) Attention, Interest, Desire, Action ❑

4. How many words have been identified as the most influential when used in marketing?
   a) 15 ❑
   b) 18 ❑
   c) 25 ❑
   d) 35 ❑

5. How should you influence a visual person?
   a) With visual evidence ❑
   b) By asking them to sing along with you in a duet ❑
   c) By using long verbal instructions ❑
   d) By being tactile with them ❑

6. What is the law of reciprocity?
   a) Seeking first to be understood, before understanding ❑
   b) If you do someone a good turn, they will naturally want to reciprocate ❑
   c) People like to be listened to, so use level 1 listening ❑
   d) Stocking up in case something runs out ❑

7. What is the law of scarcity?
   a) It means that there is plenty for everyone ❑
   b) If we think something is in short supply, we'll decide we don't want it ❑
   c) Scarcity makes a commodity less desirable ❑
   d) If we think something is in short supply, we want it ❑

8. What are emotional triggers?
   a) Small brain pulses that release a stimulus ❑
   b) External signals to stop buying ❑
   c) Appeals to feelings of guilt ❑
   d) Photos of snakes and other reptiles on your Facebook business page ❑

9. Who make the best influencers?

a) Those who talk the most ❑

b) Those who listen well ❑

c) Level 1 listeners ❑

d) Those who avoid words like good, love and new ❑

10. Why should you listen attentively?

a) To find out whether the other person is using influential words ❑

b) To pick up another person's 'cues' and then match to them in order to influence ❑

c) To indicate that you have a strong character and you will not allow the other person to leave until they have agreed to your proposal ❑

d) To avoid having to say anything ❑

7 × 7

1 Seven quotes by influential people

- 'Be the change you wish to see in the world.' Mahatma Gandhi
- 'Keep away from small people who try to belittle your ambitions. Small people always do that, but the really great make you feel that you, too, can become great.' Mark Twain
- 'Logic will get you from A to B. Imagination will take you everywhere.' Albert Einstein
- 'If you look at what you have in life, you'll always have more. If you look at what you don't have in life, you'll never have enough.' Oprah Winfrey
- 'Our greatest weakness lies in giving up. The most certain way to succeed is always to try just one more time.' Thomas Edison
- 'I like things to happen; and if they don't happen, I like to make them happen.' Winston Churchill
- 'You don't learn to walk by following rules. You learn by doing, and by falling over.' Richard Branson

2 Seven key ideas to become more influential

- Become a blogger and share your expertise; position yourself as a trusted resource. Blogs create the perfect environment for an influential, interactive relationship. Think of it as your own public relations forum. An additional benefit is it may generate actual PR. Business bloggers often receive requests for interviews or quotes from journalists who consider them industry experts.
- Develop an influential charisma. How do respected world-class leaders generate a positive impact when making

speeches? Watch their body language, gestures, style of speaking, pauses for effect, etc and experiment with replicating them for yourself.

- Think of your last significant purchase. What exactly influenced your buying decision? Was it how the product/ service was marketed? The written word? Maybe the spoken word? Was it a word-of-mouth recommendation from someone you trust? What can you learn and adopt from these sources of influence?
- Carry out a regular 'shoe review'. The smartest outfit can be let down by scuffed, dirty shoes. Invest 20 minutes at the weekend to clean the shoes you will be wearing in the coming week. If they still don't look smart after cleaning, it's time to turn them out.
- Make a list of famous, influential people that you admire and then check your local library for their biographies and autobiographies. For each one you read, jot down five key elements that contributed to their success, e.g. beliefs, values, strategies, decisions, etc. Then create a written plan to adopt as many of these proven traits as possible for yourself.
- Continually review and expand your networks, both informal (friends of friends) and formal (networking groups). The opportunities for being influential are unlimited when you network regularly.
- Social media provides a huge opportunity to be influential. On Facebook, join groups with which you have a shared interest. Start by following discussions and contributing short comments. Then build up to initiating discussions and eventually, starting up groups of your own.

3 Seven tips for making influential presentations

- Remember that feeling nervous is normal – in fact you need adrenaline to make a 'sharp' presentation. Everyone gets butterflies when presenting but it's the professionals who can get them to fly in formation!

- The symptoms associated with nervousness are identical to those associated with excitement, e.g. racing heart, sweaty palms, dry mouth. Instead of telling yourself that you are nervous, substitute the word 'excited' and you will feel quite different.
- If you need to read from a sheet of paper during your presentation, hold it in both hands with your hands pulling away from each other so that the paper is held taut. This prevents it from shaking and gives an impression to your audience (and to you) that you are confident and in control.
- Be a lighthouse. Make eye contact with your audience by looking around in sweeping arc-shape movements. This maintains a connection with them and there are bound to be some friendly faces looking back at you.
- Always have a glass of water to hand. Then if you experience a dry mouth or you need to pause momentarily to recover your composure, taking a sip of water fills the pause and looks completely natural.
- To avoid 'death by PowerPoint', follow the 5 × 5 rule. Use bullet points of no more than five words each, with a maximum of five bullet points per slide. Keep the overall number of slides used to just enough to support the content that you are delivering verbally.
- Practice makes permanent. The surefire way to become a confident, competent, persuasive presenter is to seek out opportunities to present and make the most of them. Toastmasters is a non-profit organization developing public speaking and leadership skills through practice and feedback in local clubs. For further details, check out their website at www.toastmasters.org

4 Seven ways to be a more influential networker

- When you introduce yourself at a networking event, say your first name twice to make it more memorable, e.g. 'My name is Alex, Alex Smith.'

- It is very easy to forget someone's name shortly after being introduced because your mind is busy processing your initial perception of them. When you know you are about to hear a name for the first time, 'prime' your memory by saying to yourself, 'I am about to hear this person's name and I *will* remember it.'
- Always have an 'elevator pitch' prepared. This is a very short statement, one minute long at most, that describes what you do in terms of how you help your clients successfully overcome their business challenges. This generates far more interest than just saying your name, job role and where you work.
- At networking events, it is essential to mingle and then keep moving around and introducing yourself to as many people as possible. Ensure that you maintain a genuine interest in the people you are meeting and always be seeking mutually beneficial collaboration opportunities.
- Collect business cards from everyone you speak to and then follow up with a personalized e-mail within 24 hours. If you jot down a few words on the cards relating to each person, then you can incorporate that into your e-mail and thus generate the personal touch.
- When someone tells you about their business, ask how you could identify their ideal client with a view to brokering a beneficial introduction. This will almost certainly invoke the Law of Reciprocation and they will be thinking about what they can do for you.
- If you identify a collaboration opportunity, ask the other person whether you can schedule a time for a 'coffee on the phone' chat. This assumes that at some time, probably around 11 am, they will pause for a coffee and in those few minutes, there is an opportunity for the two of you to explore mutually beneficial opportunities over the telephone. This is less 'in your face' than asking a busy person for a face to face meeting and they will respect you for that. If the conversation goes well, then they are far more likely to be amenable to a follow-up meeting.

5 Seven things at which the best social media influencers excel

- They persevere and put in the time that is needed. They understand that nobody gets famous overnight and they are prepared to spend countless hours on social media building their brands and their influence.
- They become the 'go-to' source of valuable content. They get to know their followers and share content that will benefit them. Influencers always keep their audience in mind when they post.
- They use social media to help others rather than to promote themselves. And yet in doing this, they have provided value and a service, and have thus indirectly promoted themselves.
- They contribute to the social media community whenever possible. They engage with the people who connect with them, and give back, thereby positioning themselves as a direct source of valuable knowledge and support.
- They only post positive comments. They never use social media to criticize, condemn or complain. This generates a very positive perception and increases followers.
- They consistently post high-quality content and in doing so, build a high quality reputation for themselves. They are seen as experts in their field.
- They recognize that whilst none of these things is difficult, consistency and constant focus are required and they are committed to provide these in bucketfuls.

6 Seven things to avoid

- Being 'needy'. Avoid being so focused on the outcome of a situation that it takes on the drama of a being a life or death scenario – it repels people.
- Being over confident. Even if everything has been going well during a persuasive conversation, never assume that the outcome is a foregone conclusion. People can be very unpredictable.

- Being a quitter. You must be prepared to be patient in order to achieve your outcomes. Many people need to take time to consider their decisions and just because they haven't said 'yes' yet doesn't mean that they won't. Countless goals are abandoned so close to their successful achievement because of impatience with the process.
- Being a 'limpet' – holding on to a situation that you believe you are influencing positively but in reality, is never going to come good. It is far better to recognize that you have done your best but that other influences outside of your control are determining the outcome and it is time to leave.
- Losing control and your temper when things aren't going how you want them to, and in particular, when there is a personality conflict. Even if you are in the right, you will not look good if you have allowed yourself to get drawn into a volatile situation.
- Talking more than listening. You have two ears and one mouth and it is essential you use them in that proportion. When you really listen to others, you gain insights into what is important to them and clues as to how they are most likely to be influenced.
- Making assumptions – there will always be at least a 50 per cent chance that your assumption is incorrect. Never attempt to persuade or influence someone based on an assumption. Check it out first for accuracy.

7 Seven best resources

- Holly Weeks' *Failure to Communicate: How Conversations Go Wrong and What You Can Do To Right Them* (Harvard Business Press, 2010). Difficult conversations cause stress and jangle nerves. This book serves as a reference for leaders from every profession.
- Dr Robert Cialdini's *Influence: The Psychology of Persuasion* explores the six universal principles of persuasion and how to use them to become a skilled persuader.
- Roger Fisher and William Ury's *Getting to Yes: Negotiating an Agreement without Giving In* has been in print for over 30 years and has helped countless people achieve win/win agreements both at work and in their private lives.

- Website http://www.businessballs.com is an invaluable resource for up-to-date thinking on business training and personal development in a business environment.
- http://www.theinvisiblegorilla.com/gorilla_experiment.html is a video clip that demonstrates how easily we can be influenced by our intuition into not seeing something obvious that is right in front of us.
- Daniel Pink's *Drive: The Surprising Truth About What Motivates Us* is an exploration of the secrets of high performance and personal satisfaction at work and at home.
- Sally Hogshead in *Fascinate: Your 7 Triggers to Persuasion and Captivation* promotes the concept that fascination is one of the most powerful ways to attract attention and influence behaviour, and explains how companies can use these concepts to make their products and ideas irresistible to consumers.

Answers

Lesson 1: 1b; 2a; 3d; 4b; 5a; 6b; 7a; 8c; 9b; 10a

Lesson 2: 1c; 2a; 3d; 4b; 5a; 6a; 7a; 8b; 9c; 10a

Lesson 3: 1c; 2a; 3d; 4a; 5a; 6d; 7c; 8b; 9b; 10b

Lesson 4: 1a; 2d; 3c; 4a; 5d; 6a; 7b; 8c; 9a; 10c

Lesson 5: 1a; 2a; 3d; 4b; 5a; 6b; 7b; 8c; 9d; 10a

Lesson 6: 1c; 2c; 3a; 4b; 5a; 6b; 7b; 8d; 9c; 10a

Lesson 7: 1c; 2a; 3d; 4a; 5a; 6b; 7d; 8c; 9b; 10b

About the author

Di McLanachan is managing director of Learning Curves Personal Development Ltd. She is an international trainer, executive coach, a master practitioner of Neuro-linguistic Programming and author of the bestselling book *NLP for Business Excellence*. She has frequently been featured on both radio and television, and has been delivering training in customer care on a regular basis since 1993. www.learningcurves.co.uk

Notes